Annabel**Karmel's**
Small Helpings

Annabel**Karmel's**
Small Helpings

Over 200 delicious healthy recipe ideas
for babies, toddlers and children

EBURY PRESS
LONDON

3 5 7 9 10 8 6 4 2

First published in 1994 by BBC Books

This revised edition published in 1998 by Ebury Press
Random House · 20 Vauxhall Bridge Road · London SW1V 2SA

Random House Australia (Pty) Limited
20 Alfred Street, Milsons Point · Sydney · New South Wales 2061 · Australia

Random House New Zealand Limited
18 Poland Road · Glenfield · Auckland 10 · New Zealand

Random House South Africa (Pty) Limited
Endulini · 5a Jubilee Road · Parktown 2193 · South Africa

Random House Canada
1265 Aerowood Drive · Mississauga · Ontario L4W 1B9

Random House Group Limited Reg No. 954009

www.randomhouse.co.uk

A CIP catalogue for this book is available from the British Library

0 09 186373 2

Designed by Annette Peppis/Martin Lovelock · Illustrations by Sally Davis

Colour reproduction by Colorlito, Milan

Printed in Hong Kong

Papers used by Ebury Press are natural recyclable products made from wood grown in sustainable forests.

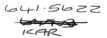

CONTENTS

INTRODUCTION

I am the mother of three young children – Nicholas, Lara and Scarlett – and like any other mother I wanted to give them the best possible start in life

Young children are most in need of a nutritious diet for their growing bodies and the quality of food fed to babies is critical to their health not only as babies but also later in life. Research has shown that a poor diet in early life can lead to bad health and impaired mental development in adulthood. Recent research by a team led by Professor Alan Lucas in Cambridge suggests that feeding breast milk rather than formula milk to premature babies for as short a period as four weeks at a time of maximum growth can influence IQ. Almost 25 per cent of young children in this country suffer from a deficiency in iron. Iron deficiency anaemia in young children can lead to permanently impaired mental development. Coronary heart disease is the major cause of death in the UK and there is little doubt that the disease process is often related to diet and can begin in childhood.

It can be proved that early feeding influences do matter to long term health. Babies cannot choose what they eat for themselves and young children do not understand the importance of good nutrition so we as parents must take on that responsibility. As attitudes towards food are established in childhood it is vitally important to establish a healthy diet from an early age.

The long lists of nutritional information on commercial baby foods look impressive but water and thickeners are often used to bulk out the ingredients and some products contain unnecessary additives like malto dextrin which is the gummy substance that can be found on the back of postage stamps! There is absolutely no doubt – and baby food manufacturers will be the first to agree – that nothing is better for your baby than freshly prepared food and making baby food yourself is cheaper than buying it in jars. There is such a lot of mystique surrounding baby foods that, when Nicholas was born, I thought that a jar of apple purée had some special ingredients and was somehow better for my baby than if I cooked and puréed apples myself.

I know that many mothers feel that they just don't have the time or the required skills but making baby food at home is simple. You don't need lots of special equipment and in just a couple of hours you can prepare a whole month's food supply for your baby.

I have written this book on the premise that a recipe has to be easy or a busy mum won't make it. All the recipes can be prepared without spending hours in the kitchen and all use fresh natural ingredients. The emphasis is on cooking for the whole family and many of the purées I made for my babies were so tasty that I often made extra large quantities and the rest of the family would get a delicious soup for supper!

Throughout this book there are many handy time-saving tips and lots of advice for all stages of your child's development to get you through the difficult times. Believe me, I've been there – Nicholas went through a stage of just not eating, Lara (my little junk food addict) would only eat provided all her food was covered with a blanket of tomato ketchup and Scarlett likes to eat everything in sight even if its not food – but then she's only one!

There are recipes for all occasions from delicious everyday meals, healthy snacks and packing your child's lunch-box to entertaining 20 hungry children at a birthday party. Nearly all the recipes can be frozen so that you can have a ready supply of healthy, home-made convenience foods in your freezer.

I hope this book will prove a treasure trove of ideas when it comes to feeding your child and will help to establish a healthy eating pattern for the rest of his life. You will be reassured to know that every recipe has been tested by a panel of small people who were never hesitant to show me exactly what they thought if they weren't impressed!

BASIC NUTRITION

Government health messages tell us we should cut down on fats (especially saturated ones), added sugars and salt. It should be possible to achieve a low-fat, low-sugar diet as recommended by the age of five years. This has been taken into consideration when devising the recipes – all of them use minimum amounts of sugar, fat and salt. As a general rule, though, it's useful to bear the following guidelines in mind when preparing food for your child.

◆ SALT: Don't add extra salt at table. Use none or very small amounts in recipes. Try using herbs for flavour instead.

◆ FAT: Butter contains mainly saturated fat; polyunsaturated margarines can be used in the recipes if preferred. Semi-skimmed milk can be used in place of whole milk and Greek yoghurt or fromage frais in place of cream.

◆ SUGAR: Try to sweeten things with pure fruit juice as there is less chance of over-sweetening. Don't use artificial sweeteners in foods or drinks.

IRON

The most important nutrient for babies and toddlers is iron. Iron deficiency is perhaps the most common nutritional problem in young children in the West and will leave your child feeling tired and run-down. As I mentioned in my Introduction, iron is an important factor in brain development and an early deficiency in iron may have a profound influence on learning development. On average, babies are born with only sufficient iron reserves in their liver to meet their needs until they double their birthweight or for approximately the first six months of life.

The iron in breast milk can be easily absorbed and infant and follow-on formulas also contain good quantities of iron. It is therefore best to continue with one of these for the first year.

It is important to select iron-rich weaning foods even if your baby is given iron-fortified milk in the first year. Introducing the right diet early on should encourage your baby to include these foods in his daily diet as he grows older, especially once he is drinking ordinary cow's milk which is a poor source of iron.

Some forms of iron are not as well absorbed into our bodies as others. Iron in foods of animal origin is better absorbed than iron in foods of plant origin. So your child will benefit more from the iron in red meat than by eating large quantities of iron-enriched breakfast cereal. Liver and offal are the richest natural sources of iron. Liver is an excellent food for young babies, it is easily digested and makes a very smooth purée. Liver pâté, however, should not be given to babies under one year because of the danger of listeriosis.

Iron present in vegetables, cereals and other non-animal forms is better absorbed by our bodies if vitamin C is consumed at the same meal. Good sources of vitamin C are fresh fruits and vegetables, particularly citrus fruits. Some infant cereals are fortified with iron and it is a good idea to mix fruit and vegetable purées rich in vitamin C with them. This will also help to thicken the consistency of some of your purées.

Foods which provide a good source of iron:
liver and kidney
red meat
egg yolk
kidney beans
lentils
dark green vegetables like spinach
dried fruit, especially dried apricots and prunes
wholegrain cereals (many of these are also fortified with iron)
oily fish like mackerel or salmon

Iron-rich foods for babies over six months are:
puréed liver and potato
chicken and chicken livers in gravy
puréed vegetables with sieved egg yolk
lentil and vegetable purée
dried apricots with iron-fortified baby rice or Weetabix and milk
spinach and potato purée

Some ideas for snacks which are rich in iron are:
chopped liver and egg sandwiches
egg and watercress
peanut butter and raisin sandwiches ** N**
dried apricots*
prunes*
dried figs*
turkey chunks (dark meat)

* Eat with a good vitamin C source, e.g. oranges, cantaloupe melon, to improve absorption of the iron they contain.

CALCIUM

MILK AND MILK PRODUCTS

Dairy foods provide the best source of calcium which is important for healthy bones and teeth. Most babies have a diet based on milk for the first year but you may not know that during adolescence we need even more calcium than younger children and adults. That's because calcium is a major component of bones and almost half of your adult bone mass is formed during adolescence. So make sure that your child gets the calcium he needs between the ages of 11 and 18. Two thirds of a pint of milk a day provides adequate calcium between one and five years.

The following foods contain the same calcium as 300 ml (10 fl oz) of milk:

40 g (1½ oz)	*Cheddar cheese*
50 g (2 oz)	*Mozzarella cheese*
200 g (7 oz)	*yoghurt*
250 g (9 oz)	*custard*
63 g (2⅓ oz)	*tofu*
450 g (1 lb)	*cottage cheese*
250 g (9 oz)	*ice-cream*
50 g (2 oz)	*sardines*

FATS

Children are very active and need energy-giving food. However, their stomachs are small so meals should not be too bulky. Fat is important as it provides the most concentrated supply of energy and thus reduces the bulk of the diet. Young children need a higher proportion of fat in their diet than adults do in order to get the energy they need from their food. Remember that babies should be quite fat until they start using up a reasonable amount of energy in walking (around 18 months). Nature's intended food, breast milk, contains about 50 per cent fat and it is better absorbed by infants than the fat in milks of other mammals. The big question is which are the best types of fat for our children?

There are two main types of fat: **saturated** and **unsaturated**. Saturated fats (in butter, cheese, milk and other dairy products, and in meat and meat products like lard, suet and dripping) tend to raise blood cholesterol levels and increase the risk of heart disease. Unsaturated fats (in oils of vegetable origin, like sunflower oil, and in polyunsaturated margarine and oily fish) tend to decrease cholesterol levels. However, the risk of heart disease in later life resulting from eating saturated fat in the first five years of life is negligible compared to a nutritional deficiency due to a marked reduction in dairy fat, so there is no need to restrict your child eating foods like cheese and dairy products. But it is best to give lean meat and get into the habit of using unsaturated fats for cooking.

Whole milk is also an exception to the guidelines on saturated fats as children under the age of two should certainly drink whole milk and not skimmed milk. The essential vitamins A and D, present in whole milk, are fat-soluble and therefore lost in the skimming process. Low-fat dairy produce is also not appropriate for very young children. Within a balanced diet semi-skimmed milk is all right from two to three years.

CARBOHYDRATES

Carbohydrates and fats provide our body with their main source of energy. There are two types of carbohydrate: **sugar** and **starch**.

Most nutritionists would like to see bread, and other cereals and vegetables which are all forms of starch, providing an increasing proportion of our carbohydrate intake. Unlike most starch-containing foods, sugar has no nutritional value other than providing energy and it is the major cause of dental decay in children's teeth. So, whenever possible, children should take sugar in a natural form (you can sweeten foods by adding fruit juice) and not in refined products like biscuits and cakes. Don't be misled: honey is just as bad as sugar; and glucose, dextrose and sucrose are simply other names for sugar.

☑️

EAT MORE

❌

EAT LESS

Starch	
wholegrain breakfast cereals	*refined, sugar-coated breakfast cereals*
brown bread and brown flour	*white bread and white flour*
wholegrain rice	*white rice*
beans and lentils	*biscuits and cakes*
pasta	

Sugar	
fruit	*soft drinks*
vegetables	*jellies*
	sugar and honey

PROTEIN

Most of us eat more protein than we need and protein deficiency is almost unheard of in the UK. Your baby doesn't need large amounts especially while he is still having a lot of milk as milk is a good source of protein.

Proteins are needed for the growth and repair of our bodies and are made up of different amino acids. Some foods – meat, poultry, fish, dairy produce, including cheese and yoghurt, and soya beans – are 'complete' proteins and contain all the amino acids that are essential to our bodies. Other foods like wholegrain cereals, bread, pulses, nuts and seeds, enriched pastas, brown rice and peanut butter are 'incomplete' proteins which provide some of the protein elements essential for good nutrition. These foods are also good because they tend to be inexpensive.

WATER

When my son Nicholas was a baby, the last drink I thought of giving him was water. Twenty eight million pounds' worth of baby drinks are sold each year in the UK and I suppose I was fooled into thinking that all the soothing herbal teas and vitamin-enriched fruit drinks were better for him. It was only when I examined their contents more closely that I discovered that most of these baby drinks were no better than sugary water.

Milk provides all the nutrients that young babies need and offering other drinks may well reduce your baby's appetite for milk. So, unless the weather is particularly hot, many babies need drink nothing other than milk.

As your baby grows older and eats more solid food, his need for water will become greater. It is a good idea to get your baby accustomed to water at an early age, once he has acquired a taste for sweet fruit drinks and herbal teas, it may be too late. A good idea is to give water when you first introduce a cup (around 8 months). The novelty of the cup may encourage your baby to drink water.

Bottles should not be made up with mineral water: it is not bacteriologically safe unless boiled and some mineral waters contain high levels of sodium and phosphate. Boiled, cooled tap water is best as it usually contains fluoride which helps to strengthen teeth.

VITAMINS

If a baby or child is eating a good balanced diet, there is no need for vitamin supplements and my opinion is that these are given more for the parent's peace of mind than for the benefit of the child.

Some nutrients can be stored in the body – these are mainly the fat-soluble vitamins A, D, E and K. They only have to be eaten once or twice a week. Other nutrients, particularly the water-soluble vitamins of the B group and vitamin C, are not really stored and should be eaten every day.

Some vitamins (and minerals) can be lost during cooking if you are not careful. Vitamin C is destroyed by heat, so don't overcook vegetables. Some of the B vitamins can leak out of the food into the cooking water so it will help if you use some of the cooking liquid to make a sauce or gravy (for example, a cheese sauce if you are making cauliflower cheese). Try to give your child raw vegetables sometimes. Otherwise it is best to steam them.

If you have no fresh vegetables or fruits, then the next best to choose are the frozen variety. In fact, some frozen foods which are frozen immediately after they are picked can be even fresher than foods that have been kept in your larder for several days (see page 69).

WHAT MAKES A BALANCED DIET?

A healthy diet for adults isn't always quite right for growing children. Children need a lot of energy-giving foods as they have small stomachs and so can only eat small amounts of food at a time. They need food that is high in energy without being too filling, otherwise they'll fill up on bulky high-fibre foods before they've eaten enough calories and nutrients. There are **four** basic food groups that are important to your child's diet from which you should try to include roughly a certain number of portions each day:

◆ MILK AND DAIRY PRODUCTS
The recommended daily number of servings is related to the age of the individual.

Babies up to 6 months: 4×225 ml (8 fl oz) bottles.
6 to 9 months: at least 600 ml (1 pint) each day.
Children: 3 servings per day.
Teenagers: 4 servings per day.

1 serving = 150 ml (5 fl oz) or 1 cup (see page 10 for equivalents).

◆ FRUITS AND VEGETABLES
Four or more servings per day (preferably one serving vitamin C rich fruit each day and a dark green leafy or a yellow vegetable every other day).

◆ MEAT AND MEAT ALTERNATIVES
Two or more servings per day.

◆ BREADS AND CEREALS

Four or more servings of wholegrain or enriched breads or cereals per day.

When solids are first introduced, you don't need to worry about a balanced diet as your baby will be getting everything she needs from her milk. However, good habits should start early, so around 6–8 months try to work towards giving your baby a properly balanced diet.

MILK AND MILK PRODUCTS

Milk and milk products provide calcium, protein and vitamin D. The Department of Health, however, advises that soft cheeses such as Brie should not be given to babies under a year because of the danger of listeriosis. Babies need whole-milk dairy products to get the energy they need and if your child isn't very keen on drinking milk, then yoghurt, cheese, creamed soup or even quality ice-creams are all good sources of milk. Remember, though, that cow's milk is a poor source of iron, so don't let your child drink so much milk that he has no appetite for solids which will provide iron in his diet. The recommended maximum amount for children over one year is 600 ml (1 pint).

FRUITS AND VEGETABLES

These foods are high in carbohydrates and contribute fibre and vitamins A, C and E to the diet as well as important minerals like potassium, calcium and iron. Try to include fruits or vegetables which are a good source of vitamin C and A every day. One of the best things you can do for your children is to get them interested in fruits and vegetables at an early age.

VITAMIN C FOODS

Citrus fruits, cantaloupe melon, apricots, kiwi fruit, papaya, cauliflower, Brussels sprouts, cabbage, tomatoes, peppers, berry fruits.

VITAMIN A FOODS

Sweet potato, carrots, cantaloupe melon, apricots, peas, broccoli, dark green leafy vegetables.

MEAT AND MEAT ALTERNATIVES

Red meat should now be quite safe to give to babies. If you still have some concerns, then buy muscle meat (joints, chops, steaks, etc) and mince it yourself rather than buying meat that is already minced. Meat provides protein, iron, zinc and vitamin B12.

Red meat and liver provide the best source of iron for your child and if your child is drinking a lot of cow's milk and eating mainly low-iron content foods then iron deficiency anaemia may occur. See the section on iron (page 8) to help you choose foods and recipes which are good sources of iron.

Even without red meat most children eating a good varied diet will get the protein they need from alternative sources like chicken, fish, eggs, seeds, grains, tofu, pulses and nuts, even peanut butter. Egg yolks are packed with calcium and phosphorus for building and maintaining strong bones and teeth, and are a good source of iron. However, soft cooked eggs should not be given to babies under a year because of the danger of salmonella.

BREADS AND CEREALS

These foods provide iron, niacin, thiamine and fibre. Choose wholegrain and enriched breads and cereals for your child – granary bread, wholewheat pasta, brown rice, porridge. Niacin and thiamine are both B vitamins, vital for energy, emotional balance and important for hair, skin and nails.

Recently there has been a lot of concern over the lack of fibre in the Western diet, but in the case of babies and young children, care needs to be taken not to include too much fibre. High-fibre foods tend to be bulky and young children may feel full up before they can eat enough to get sufficient nutrients and energy. Some types of fibre, like wheat bran, also contain substances that interfere with the body's absorption of vitamins and minerals. So choose foods like wholemeal bread and wholegrain breakfast cereals in your child's diet but avoid foods with added fibre and don't add bran to young children's food.

VEGETARIAN AND VEGAN DIETS

Parents who follow a vegetarian diet are often worried that this might be unsuitable for their baby. In fact a vegetarian diet which includes egg, milk and dairy products is a perfectly good diet for babies. All animal protein, including egg and milk, is a high-quality protein. Cereal and vegetable protein has a lower quality, although the protein from pulses (peas, beans, nuts and lentils) is almost as good as animal protein.

In order for your child to get a high-quality protein at each meal, you should include some dairy food – it need only be a small quantity – or combine different non-animal proteins together (for example, cereal and vegetable protein at the same meal, such as peas and baby rice, Rice is nice [page 75] or Tasty tofu [page 78]).

A vegan diet, excluding all animal foods, may pose some difficulties for a young baby. Large quantities of bulky cereals, vegetables and pulses need to be eaten in order to provide enough nutrients, and young babies are not able to consume these large amounts of food.

Of course if the baby is being breast-fed then it will be getting very good quality protein from its mother's milk. After breast-feeding has stopped then it is advisable for vegan babies to take a specially adapted infant soya formula (adult milks are not suitable). At least a pint of this should be taken up to the age of at least one year and preferably beyond this.

One particular B vitamin is only found in animal foods and this is vitamin B12. It should be present in breast milk and the special soya milks also contain plenty. But if these foods are not included in the diet then a supplement needs to be given. Vegetarians and in particular vegan babies can also suffer a deficiency in iron. Some vegetable foods such as beans and dark green vegetables contain iron but you need to give a vitamin C rich food (e.g. orange segments) with them as this helps absorption.

FOOD ALLERGIES

Everybody is equipped with an immune system and when a foreign body like a measles virus gets inside us, our body manufactures a specific killing substance called an antibody to beat off the invader. This defence works well to fight off disease, however, sometimes our body might identify a fairly harmless substance like a particular food as being a dangerous foreigner and create large amounts of antibodies. This can result in unpleasant side effects. A **food reaction** is generally short-lived and not the same as a true **food allergy** which involves the immune system. The symptoms of food intolerance can manifest itself in several different ways: vomiting, diarrhoea, abdominal pain, nausea, asthma, eczema and swelling. The only treatment available for a true food allergy is to avoid the problem food.

There is an enormous amount of anxiety about food allergies which makes mothers nervous when it comes to feeding their babies. However, unless there is a family history, food allergies affect only a very small minority of babies. Food intolerance is very difficult to diagnose and symptoms like diarrhoea, colic and skin rashes can be misdiagnosed as a food allergy.

If there is no history of allergy in the family and your child has a mild reaction to a particular food, it doesn't mean that you should never give that food to your child again. By regularly eating small portions of that food your baby may in time build up antibodies. Many children outgrow early allergies to food by the age of three and there is no evidence that delaying the introduction of foods such as eggs or wheat until after six months will prevent allergy, except in high-risk babies.

High-risk babies are those where there is a family history of what is called **atopic** disease – hay-fever, asthma, eczema and so on. In this case there are almost certainly advantages in breast-feeding for at least four to six months and in not introducing foods such as cow's milk, eggs and wheat–

based products until after six months, by which time the baby's own immune system has had time to mature.

Breast milk is the best choice for babies sensitive to cow's milk. However, the breast-feeding mother may need to limit the amount of dairy products she eats or she may inadvertently pass them through her milk to her baby.

There has been a trend for parents to give soya milks in the hope of preventing allergic disease or if their baby is showing allergic symptoms. I think there is little point in this. Soya milk does not prevent the development of allergy, even in high-risk babies, nor is it a particularly effective treatment for milk allergy. Almost as many babies are allergic to soya milks as are to cow's milk and soya milks inhibit the absorption of certain key minerals including iron.

Ideally, high-risk babies should be breast-fed for at least 6 months when possible.

My advice is that if you suspect that your baby is allergic, don't be in a hurry to take foods out of the diet. Try the food on several occasions. If you are getting the same symptoms each time then you should seek advice from a dietitian, especially if removing an important food such as milk or wheat. It may be better in the long run to accept minor symptoms rather than take a major decision which might result in nutritional deficiencies.

The commonest foods which can sometimes carry a risk of allergic reactions are cow's milk and dairy products, eggs, fish (especially shellfish) and nuts (see below).

Much has been made of withholding gluten (wheat-based products) until six months, but there is no scientific proof that withholding it after the age of four months reduces the chances of developing an allergy. If there is a family history of gluten intolerance, then you should definitely seek medical advice as this can induce coeliac disease which, although rare, can be very serious. Gluten is found in wheat, rye, barley and oats. As flour and bread are such staple elements in our diet, the exclusion of gluten would mean a considerable change. However, cornflour, potato flour, tapioca, rice and buckwheat spaghetti are all safe for your baby.

Honey should not be given to children under one year as it can contain bacteria that may cause infant botulism.

NUTS

Nuts can cause a severe allergic reaction. Where there is a history of food allergy, avoid all products containing nuts until the child is about three years old. Where there is no history of allergy, peanut butter can be given after the age of one year. Any recipe containing nuts in this book is labelled with an **N**.

THE MILLION DOLLAR SMILE

Cutting teeth can be a jolly painful business, but I often wonder whether teething is worse for the grizzly baby or the parents who are kept up all night. When the teeth do arrive, parents bully their children into regular brushing only to find that around the age of seven, these prized white pearls become the property of the tooth fairy!

Visiting the dentist should hold no fears for a child with healthy teeth and he should love brandishing his 'Mickey Mouse' toothbrush and 'I've been to the dentist' smiling crocodile sticker, looking forward to his next visit. If we encourage good dental hygiene and control our child's diet successfully, establishing good eating habits early on, then there is no reason why your child should ever have any tooth decay.

Cultivating a sweet tooth is easy but taming one is a Leviathan task. Bad habits start early. Although a drink with a meal won't do much harm, sometimes toddlers are given sweetened drinks in a bottle or a beaker to carry around and it goes into their mouth dozens of times a day. Leaving your baby to suck on a bottle of fruit juice at naptime or bedtime is asking for trouble. Not only is there the risk of choking, but at night there's little saliva in the mouth to wash the acid in the juice away and your baby could develop 'nursing bottle syndrome' which occurs when the upper front teeth are decayed by the liquid that bathes them whilst your child is sleeping. When putting your young child to bed, use only water in the bottle. Even milk contains lactose which is a form of sugar. As soon as your child is ready, wean him off bottles altogether.

Encourage your child to enjoy eating a wide variety of fruit for pudding instead of sugary desserts. It is worth taking a little time to present the fruit attractively to entice him. Calcium-rich foods like cheese, yoghurt, milk and nuts are important for strong, healthy teeth. Do not bribe your child with the promise of sweets or ice-cream if he is good and similarly do not offer him a sticky bun if he finishes all his spinach. How about giving **good** food as treats instead of **bad** ones?

About one third of the children in this country will have had cavities in their teeth before the age of five. It is the *frequency* with which children consume sugary foods that does the most damage. A chocolate bar eaten in one go is much better than a packet of sweets sucked one at a time for hours on end. If you want to give your little one sweet treats, then give them at mealtimes when there is plenty of saliva in the mouth as this will help to 'wash' the teeth clean. Young children need to eat snacks, they cannot always eat enough food at mealtimes to get all the nutrients and energy they need. Use your imagination and offer your child raw vegetables with a tasty dip or cheese with fruit (see the chapter Scrumptious Snacks).

Probably 50 per cent of our sugar intake is in the form of 'hidden sugars' in manufactured foods and drinks like tomato ketchup, breakfast cereals, raisins or soft drinks – a tin of spaghetti in tomato sauce contains 3 teaspoons of sugar.

Many people believe that young children are bound to have some fillings, yet with a combination of careful plaque removal and a reduction in the amount and frequency of sugar at and between meals, decay can be prevented completely. Every time sugar meets plaque on teeth, acid is produced and nearly all foods contain sugar in one form or another.

You should start brushing your child's teeth as soon as the first tooth is through. With careful brushing at least twice a day you can dislodge the bacteria which reacts with the sugar to cause decalcification so that decay cannot take place. Children don't have the fine control needed to clean their teeth properly until they are about five. Avoid spreading your child's toothbrush with a great dollop of toothpaste, a small pea-sized ball at the end of the brush is quite sufficient.

Fluoride helps to strengthen tooth enamel and is one of the most effective elements in preventing tooth decay. There are many ways in which you can ensure that your child gets adequate fluoride protection, like drinking tap water, brushing with fluoride toothpaste or taking fluoride tablets or drops. Too much fluoride, however, can cause discoloration of the teeth so it is best to consult your dentist before giving fluoride supplements.

BABIES

INTRODUCING SOLIDS

WHEN TO WEAN

For all babies, solids should not be introduced before the age of four months because the protective factors and baby's immune system which help prevent allergy are not sufficiently developed. With the later introduction of solids at six months, allergic reactions to food are less likely in high-risk infants. However, leaving the introduction of solids much later than six months is not a good idea as babies should start to get used to swallowing food, which, unlike sucking is not a natural reflex and they should be starting to explore new tastes and textures. After all a world without food would be a pretty dull place!

Your baby will probably let you know when he is ready to start solids – he may still be hungry after a 250-ml (8-oz) bottle or need more frequent breast-feeds, he may become more unsettled at night or the interval between feeds may become shorter and shorter. A good indication that she's ready for solids is when your baby starts showing a great interest in your food as you eat. She may even try and grab it!

The first solids are introduced to get your baby used to different flavours and textures. The amount of food eaten to begin with will probably be so small that it will only make a small contribution to your baby's diet. However, introducing a taste for healthy foods early on will hopefully lead to healthy eating habits later.

MILK IS MAJOR

Milk is the most important food for the whole of the first year of life. It provides a large proportion of all nutrients and energy (calories). Therefore, the main drink for a baby should be breast milk or a specially adapted infant formula. Unmodified cow's milk is unsuitable for babies under six months as it is too high in salt and protein and it is best to continue with breast or formula milk for the first year as it is enriched with vitamins and minerals. It is

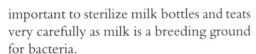

important to sterilize milk bottles and teats very carefully as milk is a breeding ground for bacteria.

At six months when babies are eating several solid meals a day, they will still need at least 600 ml (1 pint) of breast or formula milk. A baby will be getting all the protein he needs from this milk. From six months, ordinary cow's milk and its products – yoghurt, cheese and fromage frais are very useful weaning foods. However, be warned, lurking in a pot of fruit yoghurt can be up to 6 teaspoons of sugar. It is best to buy natural yoghurt or fromage frais and sweeten it with fruit purée.

Although many of us tend to choose low-fat foods these days, young children need more calories than adults since they grow very rapidly and are physically active. They also have relatively small appetites, so they really need the calorie content of full-cream milk (see also page 11 for more on this).

Follow-on milk is designed for babies of six months to a year who may be having difficulties in coping with solid foods. They contain more iron and vitamins, particularly vitamin D. However in general, a follow-on milk offers few additional benefits compared with a standard formula, so if your baby is coping well with solids, a follow-on milk isn't necessary.

Every baby is different so it is not possible to give exact quantities, however between four and six months when your baby is weaned onto solids, she should be having four or five 250-ml (8-oz) bottles of milk each day. At around six months, babies should have between 600 ml (1 pint) and 900 ml (1½ pints) of milk each day. Breast-feeding mums should ideally give around five feeds a day, but once the baby is eating more solids four feeds should be sufficient. About 450 ml (15 fl oz) a day is recommended for toddlers up to the age of two and of course you can cunningly disguise this in the form of yoghurt, fromage frais, scrambled eggs, cream soups or even ice-cream.

At around eight to ten months when your baby is able to hold objects in her hands quite well, start to give her milk in a cup (the double-handled plastic cups with weighted bases are good). Inevitably less milk will end up inside your baby and she will become more hungry for her solids.

OTHER DRINKS

If your baby is thirsty between milk feeds then offer cooled boiled water rather than sugary drinks.

For older children, too, offer water or some freshly squeezed orange juice. If you do buy cartons of juice, make sure they contain no added sugar. A carton of Ribena contains the equivalent of 8 teaspoons of sugar, a large Cola can contain 10 teaspoons of sugar and many fruit juices contain less than 10 per cent juice. These drinks will fill up your child's tummy and take away his appetite. Even pure fruit juices can be extremely sweet and contain fructose which is bad for teeth so it's best to dilute them with water before giving them to your child.

FIRST FOODS

Babies are born with a naturally sweet tooth, after all breast milk is sweet, so I prefer to introduce savoury tastes first and then move on to fruits. On pages 27 to 28 is a list of vegetables and fruits for very young babies and how to prepare them.

Shop-bought baby rice is a good first food, it is bland and easily digested and combines well with fruit and vegetable purées, water or milk. Choose one that is fortified with vitamins and minerals and be careful to check the list of ingredients to make sure there is no added sugar.

Salt should not be added to your baby's food before one year. This is because a baby's kidneys are not mature enough to cope with it. Try using herbs instead of salt to add flavour.

To begin with give your baby single ingredient purées starting with foods that have a fairly mild taste (vegetables with a slightly sweet flavour like carrots or squash are popular) and once your baby gets used to the taste of a variety of foods on their own, you can begin combining foods. (See page 31 and recipes in the chapter 6 to 9 Months on pages 34 to 42). Remember that steaming or microwaving preserve more nutrients than simmering in water.

A lot of people advise giving the same purée for three to four days and then going on to another one once you are sure there is no adverse reaction. In my experience, if you are looking for symptoms then you are almost bound to find them and there is the danger that mothers will remove foods from their baby's diet unnecessarily. Unless there is a history of allergy in the family, there is no reason why your baby shouldn't eat a variety of foods each day.

At the beginning, don't expect your baby to take more than 1-2 teaspoons of solids.

A FEW TIPS BEFORE YOU START.

◆ For the first few weeks of weaning put most foods through a mouli or blender or food processor to make sure they are really smooth and make them quite runny so that they are easy for your baby to swallow.

◆ Hygiene is paramount when it comes to preparing baby food and feeding your

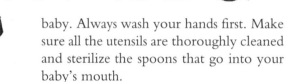

baby. Always wash your hands first. Make sure all the utensils are thoroughly cleaned and sterilize the spoons that go into your baby's mouth.

◆ Don't give your baby new foods at bed-time or you may be kept up all night coping with wind!

◆ Sometimes it is a good idea to give your baby a little milk before his solids so that he is not frantically hungry – you may find this will encourage him to be more receptive to new tastes.

◆ Buy some special weaning spoons which are shallow and make it easier for your baby to take the food with his lips. Don't be in a hurry to take the spoon out of your baby's mouth as it may take him a while to lick the food off the spoon. Never try to force your baby to eat.

◆ If your baby is not keen on certain foods, try mixing them with familiar tastes like breast or formula milk or baby rice.

◆ Don't be put off if your baby spits the food out. A natural reaction when a baby sucks is to push his tongue forward, so often the food you put in comes straight out again – don't be discouraged because it doesn't mean he dislikes the taste. Swallowing is a skill your baby will need to learn so be patient. Smile and encourage your baby, after all eating should be fun.

◆ Don't spoon food out of a bowl into your baby's mouth and then return the remainder to the fridge for the next day. Food in the bowl could become contaminated by bacteria from your baby's mouth.

◆ Make eating fun: if possible sit opposite your baby and smile and encourage her. Let her see you eating too – babies are great mimics and if they see you tucking in . . .

EQUIPMENT

You don't need to rush out and buy loads of special equipment to make your own baby food. However, it is worth investing in the following items.

◆ *MOULI*: This is a hand-turned food mill which is not expensive to buy and which gets rid of all the indigestible bits like the husks of vegetables, the skins of dried fruit, the seeds of tomatoes and can be used to make super smooth purées for your baby. It is especially useful when preparing small quantities.

◆ *BLENDER OR FOOD PROCESSOR*: Some food processors have mini attachments for making small quantities – this is particularly useful for making baby purées. Electric hand blenders are also good for making foods like apples or carrots into smooth purées. Foods with tough skins or seeds are better puréed in a mouli.

◆ *STEAMER*: Steaming foods helps to preserve nutrients and the food tastes much better as none of the flavour is lost in the cooking liquid. A multi-layered steamer is good for cooking several foods at once. I think that once you have tasted steamed vegetables, you will want to cook them that way for the whole family.

PREPARING AHEAD AND FREEZING

Who has time to fool around in the kitchen with young babies in the house you may well ask? Home-made purées should be eaten either on the day they are prepared or refrigerated and eaten the next day, but this is where a freezer becomes invaluable. In a couple of hours I can prepare a whole month's food supply for my baby. I nearly always prepare recipes in bulk and that way I have a constant supply of home-made convenience foods.

It's so simple to freeze food in ice-cube trays or little pots and, once frozen, transfer them to freezer bags. Nearly all the recipes in this book are suitable for freezing (those not suitable are marked; ❋). Cooked purées should last for between four and six months in a 4-star freezer. Always label the food with the expiry date to make sure you never give food to your baby that is past its best.

◆　Freeze food as soon as you can after it has been cooked. However, do not put warm food into the freezer, it makes your freezer work too hard and causes ice crystals to form.

◆　Freezing can dry out purées so you may have to add some liquid like milk, stock or juice when you re-heat it.

◆　If you have friends with babies roughly the same age you could prepare two or three recipes in bulk each and then swap half of your food for half of your friend's recipes thereby each spending only half as long in the kitchen.

◆　Always re-heat food thoroughly so that it is piping hot. Microwaves are great for cooking food from frozen but make sure you stir the food to get an even distribution of heat. Let the food cool down a little and test the temperature of the food yourself before giving it to your baby.

◆　Apart from banana, avocado, melon and aubergine, most fruit and vegetable purées freeze very well.

4 TO 6 MONTHS

FIRST FRUITS

APPLE AND PEAR Peel, core and cut apples into pieces. Simmer in enough water to cover or steam until soft. Ripe pears can be puréed uncooked. To microwave, chop the peeled apple, sprinkle with a little water or pure apple juice, cover and cook on full power for 3–4 minutes until soft. Purée in a blender.

BANANA AND PAPAYA These need no cooking. Peel the fruit and purée in a blender or, for older babies, mash with a fork. Add a little boiled water, pure fruit juice or breast or formula milk if the banana is too thick and sticky for your baby to swallow. Another method is to bake the banana in its skin in the oven (at gas mark 4, 350°F, 180°C) until the skin turns black, then peel and mash the banana – this brings out the sweetness in the fruit and makes it nice and soft. Be warned that some babies find banana difficult to digest.

FIRST VEGETABLES

CARROTS OR COURGETTES Baby carrots are very sweet so you could try using these sometimes. Peel, trim and slice the carrots, either steam until tender or simmer in water. Purée in a blender. If the carrots are steamed you will need to add some of the water from the steamer to make a smooth purée. It is best to steam courgettes and, since they naturally contain a lot of water, you probably won't need to add any.

To microwave courgettes or carrots, trim ends, cut into slices, sprinkle with water, cover with clear film and pierce. Courgettes will take about 3 minutes and carrots 5 minutes. Cook on full power.

POTATOES, SWEDE, PARSNIP OR SWEET POTATO Swede, parsnip and sweet potato have an appealingly sweet taste that babies love. Peel the vegetables and cut into chunks. Cover with water, bring to the boil and simmer until tender. Alternatively, you could bake the potato or sweet potato in the oven at gas mark 4, 350°F, (180°C) for about 1 hour (or until soft). Prick the skin and place on a foil-lined pan, turning after 30 minutes.

Small quantities are more economically cooked in a microwave. Prick the skin of the potato, put into a shallow microwave-proof dish and microwave on high for 7 to 9 minutes or until tender. To microwave parsnip or swede, cook with water, covered, for about 5 minutes on high. Purée in a blender, adding some of the cooking water or breast or formula milk to make a smooth purée.

BUTTERNUT SQUASH, ACORN SQUASH, PUMPKIN   There are several ways of cooking squash or pumpkin, but baking in the oven caramelizes their natural sugars and gives them the best flavour. Cut the squash in half, scoop out the seeds and brush the flesh generously with melted butter. Place on foil and bake in an oven pre-heated to gas mark 4, 350°F (180°C) for 40 minutes or until tender. If the flesh starts to dry out, cover with foil. Alternatively, proceed as above, place in a microwave-proof dish and cook on high for between 10 and 12 minutes or until soft. You could also cut squash or pumpkin into chunks, simmer in water or sauté in butter until tender.

CREAM OF FRUIT OR VEGETABLE PURÉE   Mixing fruit or vegetable purées with baby rice and milk is often a good way of introducing new foods, particularly foods with a strong taste like broccoli.

cream of pumpkin

Pumpkin is a much neglected vegetable, but I find that babies love the flavour. You could use swede here if you prefer.

175 g (6 oz) pumpkin, chopped
Knob of butter or margarine
1 tablespoon baby rice
3 tablespoons formula milk

For the best flavour I cook the pumpkin in the oven until tender (about 40 minutes at gas mark 4, 350°F, 180°C) with a little butter or margarine. Alternatively, you can sauté it in a pan until tender or simmer it in water or stock or cook it in the microwave on high for between 10 and 12 minutes.

Purée the cooked pumpkin or roughly chop. Mix the baby rice with the milk and stir into the pumpkin.

Makes 2 portions

6 TO 9 MONTHS

There will be a lot of change in your baby's life between six and nine months. She will start sitting up and will be able to sit in a high chair and she will spend many more hours awake. She will probably have cut a few teeth and she will begin to feed herself although her aim will be far from perfect. Your baby will be starting to learn to chew so you can vary the texture of her food a little more – mashing, mincing or chopping. Babies at this stage can eat between 1 and 4 tablespoons of food three times a day.

You may need to limit foods which your child might find indigestible like spinach, dried fruit, lentils, citrus and berry fruits. You can now buy lots of unusual fruits and vegetables in supermarkets like sharon fruit or acorn squash. Many of these are simple to prepare and although they may seem a little more expensive than ordinary fruits and vegetables, you can make a lot of portions from them and they are great mixed with other foods e.g. sharon fruit and fromage frais or acorn squash and apple. Although your baby will still be breast-fed or drinking formula milk, cow's milk is fine for mixing in foods and for cooking.

At around six months, chicken, fish and meat can be introduced. Chicken combines well with lots of different foods and chicken stock forms the basis of many of my recipes. Fish is good too – quick to cook and nice and soft – but take special care to check that *all* bones have been removed. Choose plaice or hake to begin with as they have the smoothest texture. Liver is probably the best meat to start with as it is very nutritious and, again, purées to a very smooth consistency.

MORE FRUITS

Remember that raw is best so try giving your baby mashed or grated fruits as soon as you think he can cope with them. Peaches, pears, papaya, banana, plums and melon can be puréed without cooking provided they are ripe.

APRICOTS   To skin, cut a shallow cross in the skin, submerge in boiling water for 1 minute and then plunge in cold water and peel. Cut the fruit into pieces and discard the stone. Simmer until soft, or steam. Or microwave on full power for 2 to 3 minutes until soft. Then purée.

MELON   Cantaloupe melons (the small pale green melon with the orange flesh) are a rich source of vitamin C and A and a good ripe honeydew melon has a sweet taste that babies love. Cut the melon in half, scoop out the seeds, cut the flesh into chunks and mash or purée. Do not freeze.

DRIED FRUIT   Dried fruit tends to have a laxative effect on young babies and prunes are good if your baby is constipated. For young babies it is a good idea to mix dried fruit purées with milk and baby rice, yogurt or fromage frais. If the dried fruit is very hard then soak in hot water for a couple of hours before cooking. Cover the fruit with water and simmer until soft (about 10 minutes). Purée in a mouli to get rid of the tough skins.

BERRY FRUITS   These can be quite indigestible for babies so give them in moderation or mixed with other fruits, e.g. banana or apple. Steam, simmer in a little water or microwave covered for about 1 minute on full power. Purée in a mouli to get rid of the seeds. Cooked berry fruits tend to be quite watery so try mixing in some baby rice to thicken the purée.

MORE VEGETABLES

BROCCOLI AND CAULIFLOWER   Wash the vegetables carefully and cut into small florets. Steam until tender and purée in a blender or mouli with some of the steaming water or milk. Alternatively, simmer in water. To cook in a microwave, sprinkle with water, cover and cook for 3 minutes on high or until tender.

GREEN BEANS   Top, tail and remove any stringy bits. If using long runner beans then cut them diagonally into about 3 pieces. Steam until tender. Alternatively microwave on high, covered, for about 3 minutes. Runner beans are best puréed in a mouli for young babies to get rid of the indigestible parts. Add a little boiled water or milk to make a smooth purée.

SPINACH   Wash the spinach leaves carefully, removing the coarse stalks, and steam until tender. Alternatively, put the leaves into a pan with just a little water (or use frozen spinach to save time). Simmer, covered, until tender. Purée in a mouli or

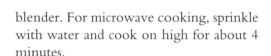

blender. For microwave cooking, sprinkle with water and cook on high for about 4 minutes.

FRESH PEAS   Steam until tender or cover fresh, podded peas or frozen peas with water and simmer until tender. Purée in a mouli to get rid of the husks and add a little of the cooking liquid or some milk to make a smooth consistency. To microwave, add a little water and cook, covered, for 3 to 4 minutes for frozen peas. Fresh peas may need a little more time.

PEPPERS   To skin peppers, cut them in half, remove the white core and seeds, flatten them with your hand and rub the skin with oil. Place under a pre-heated grill until the skin has blackened. Let cool and the skin will rub off easily. Purée with milk or cooled boiled water.

WINNING COMBINATIONS

Once your baby has been introduced to a fairly wide range of single-ingredient purées then you can start mixing foods together – below are some combinations that I have found babies like and I hope this list will give you inspiration to try some ideas of your own. A good test, of course, is to taste them yourself because if mum thinks they're delicious, chances are that baby will agree!

Don't be afraid to mix strange combinations. Adding fruit to foods that your child refuses to eat often encourages them to eat. When Lara was two, she flatly refused to eat chicken and no amount of cajoling or bribery would make her change her mind. I made up a recipe combining apples (one of her favourites) and the dreaded chicken and she kept on asking for more until there was none left. In my experience the more you want a child to eat something, the less likely they are to oblige you, so I find that this gradual introduction makes a great compromise.

APPLES OR PEARS AND . . .

cinnamon or vanilla
dried fruit, e.g. raisins, prunes, apricots and custard
yoghurt, fromage frais or sieved cottage cheese
blackberries
cereals, e.g. baby rice, oats
chicken
cottage cheese or cream cheese
butternut squash
carrots
sweet potato
blueberries
raisins and fromage frais
pumpkin or squash
plums
prunes

BANANAS AND . . .

yoghurt or fromage frais
avocado
courgette
dried fruit
kiwi
strawberry and fromage frais or yogurt
raspberry
chicken
yoghurt and honey
tangerines
papaya

SQUASH AND . . .

apples
pears
peaches
grapes
cinnamon
spinach
chicken
carrot and fromage frais

PASTA AND . . .

spinach and cheese
apples and carrots
courgettes, tomato and onions
tomato and cheese
minced meat, aubergine and tomatoes
liver, onion and mushrooms
chicken, leeks and cream
cheese sauce and vegetables

CHICKEN AND . . .

grapes with béchamel sauce
apple
rice and tomatoes
cottage cheese and pineapple or peach
avocado
green beans and apple juice
peaches and rice
potato and tomato
pumpkin and grapes

BEEF AND . . .

pasta, tomatoes and onions
carrots, potatoes and onions
liver, aubergine and tomatoes
barley and prunes
rice and mushrooms

good old-fashioned chicken stock

Chicken stock forms the basis of so many of my recipes. It's very simple to make and full of goodness for your baby. Chicken stock will keep in the fridge for two days. I use some of the chicken stock to make up into baby purées and freeze the remainder in several small containers for a wonderful clear soup. For maximum flavour I make the stock from a boiler chicken with its giblets. Otherwise a good stock can be made using the carcass from a cooked roast chicken with as many giblets as possible. If your butcher has any veal bones available these can be used to add to the flavour of the stock.

1 large boiler chicken plus giblets
2.25 litres (4 pints) water
2 large onions, peeled and roughly chopped
3 large carrots, scrubbed and roughly sliced
2 parsnips, scrubbed and roughly chopped
1 small turnip, washed and cut into chunks
2 leeks, white part only, sliced
Half a celery stalk and a handful of celery leaves
2 sprigs of parsley
1 bay leaf
2 or 3 chicken stock cubes (optional for babies over one year)

Wash the chicken and giblets, trimming away excess fat. Alternatively break up the carcass of the cooked roast chicken. Put into a large pan and cover with water. Bring to the boil slowly and remove the scum from the surface. Add all the remaining ingredients and simmer very gently for 3 hours. Remove the chicken when it is tender (after about 2 hours), strip off all the flesh (to use in other dishes) and then return the carcass to the pan. Refrigerate overnight and in the morning you can remove the layer of fat that settles on top. Simply strain for a lovely rich stock. This also makes a wonderful clear soup with some vermicelli or farfalle (bow-tie pasta).

makes about 1.75 litres (3 pints)

vegetable stock

For young babies leave out the Marmite but for older babies this will improve the flavour.

450 g (1 lb) carrots
450 g (1 lb) onions
Top half of a celery stick
1 small parsnip
½ small turnip

25 g (1 oz) butter or margarine
1 bouquet garni
A few black peppercorns
1 teaspoon Marmite
3.4 litres (6 pints) water

Peel and wash the vegetables. Dry them and slice them into big pieces and then sauté in butter or margarine over a low heat until lightly browned. Add the rest of the ingredients, pour over the water and bring to the boil. Cover and simmer for about 3 hours. Strain, allow to cool and refrigerate for several hours. Remove any fat from the top and freeze the stock in 600-ml (1-pint) containers.

makes about 2.25 litres (4 pints)

baby muesli

Combining oat flakes with milk and fruit makes a tasty nutritious breakfast for your baby. For my basic recipe I have used semi-dried apricots and fresh pear. Other good combinations are peach, pear and banana or blueberries, grated apple and apple juice. You can experiment, making your own mueslis with fresh fruit that is in season. This is good for older children, too, served hot on a cold winter's morning.

6 dried apricots
150 ml (5 fl oz) milk
15 g (¹/₂ oz) oat flakes

1 large or 2 small ripe pears, peeled,
cored and cut into pieces

Simmer the apricots in water until soft (about 4 minutes). Meanwhile, heat the milk in a saucepan, stir in the oats, bring to the boil and simmer, stirring occasionally, for 3 to 4 minutes until thickened. Once cooked, set aside. Drain and roughly chop the apricots and mix these together with the cooked oats and pear(s). Purée in a blender.

makes 4 portions

fruit purée flavoured with vanilla

Simmering fruit with a vanilla pod is a good way of adding extra sweetness without added sugar. I've added a kiwi fruit as it is a good source of vitamin C but you need a sweet ripe one. Otherwise substitute peach or pear.

1 apple, peeled, cored and thinly sliced
2 plums, peeled and cut into pieces
4 tablespoons apple juice
1 small piece of vanilla pod or a drop of
pure vanilla extract
1 ripe kiwi fruit, peeled and sliced

Simmer the apples and plums in the apple juice, together with the vanilla pod, until soft. Remove the vanilla pod and purée together with the sliced kiwi. Push through a sieve for young babies to get rid of the little black seeds.

makes 3 portions

Cinderella's pumpkin

This is one of Scarlett's favourite combinations – and it tastes so good you could make it as a soup for the rest of the family. If you can't find pumpkin, try butternut squash instead.

15 g (½ oz) butter
50 g (2 oz) white part of a leek, sliced
225 g (8 oz) pumpkin (or butternut

squash) peeled and cut into cubes
¼ pint (5 fl oz) chicken or vegetable
stock (see pages 33–4)

Melt the butter in a saucepan and sauté the leek until soft and lightly golden. Add the pumpkin and continue to cook for 2 minutes. Pour over the stock, bring to the boil and then simmer covered for 30 minutes or until the pumpkin is tender. Purée in a blender or mash with a fork for older babies.

makes 3–4 portions

butternut squash

Butternut squash is very popular with babies, simply bake in the oven, steam or microwave and then purée, adding a little milk, apple or orange juice. It combines well with lots of different fruits and vegetables and this is a winner with my baby daughter when peaches are in season. See Winning combinations (pages 31–2) for other ideas.

1 small butternut or acorn squash
25 g (1 oz) butter or margarine,
melted

¼ teaspoon cinnamon (optional)
2 peaches, skinned
Milk, stock or water to purée

Pre-heat the oven to gas mark 4, 350°F (180°C).

Cut the squash in half, scoop out the seeds, brush with melted butter or margarine and sprinkle with cinnamon, if using. Bake it until soft (about 50 minutes). Alternatively, peel, de-seed and chop the flesh and cook covered on full power in a microwave for 6 minutes. Slice the

peaches and add to the cooked butternut squash (for young babies you could steam or microwave the peaches for a couple of minutes). Purée the squash and peaches in a blender, adding a little milk or water if necessary to make a smooth purée.

makes 8 portions

broccoli trio

Potato makes a great thickener for any vegetable purées so you can experiment with new combinations using it as a base. Another good thickener is sieved hard-boiled egg yolks – they also provide a good source of iron.

1 × 225-g (8-oz) potato, peeled and chopped
50 g (2 oz) broccoli florets

1 medium courgette, sliced
1–2 tablespoons milk

Boil the potato (in the bottom of a steamer, if you have one) for about 12 minutes and steam the other vegetables for 8 to 10 minutes. Simply blend all the ingredients to the required purée.

makes 4 portions

sweet pea purée

The sautéed onions and peas give this purée a naturally sweet taste that appeals to babies.

1 tablespoon chopped onion
15 g (½ oz) butter or margarine
75 g (3 oz) courgette, topped, tailed
and sliced

75 g (3 oz) frozen peas
85 ml (3 fl oz) chicken or vegetable
stock (see pages 33–4)

Sautée the onion in the butter or margarine until soft, then add the courgette and sautée for 2 minutes. Add the peas, pour over the stock, bring to the boil and simmer for about 5 minutes until tender. Purée in a mouli or sieve.

makes 2 portions

see in the dark purée

Interestingly, cooked carrots are more nutritious than raw as the betacarotene is absorbed better into our bodies. Eating carrots improves your night vision.

2 medium carrots, scrubbed and sliced
1 apple, peeled and sliced

A knob of butter
4 tablespoons milk

Steam the carrots for 10 minutes, then add the sliced apple and continue to steam for another 10 minutes or until the carrots are soft. Purée the carrots and apple together with a knob of butter and the milk until smooth.

makes 4 portions

chicken with winter vegetables

This makes a lovely smooth-textured purée.

100 g (4 oz) chicken, cut into pieces
½ tablespoon chopped onion
15 g (½ oz) celery, chopped
15 g (½ oz) leek, chopped
1 medium carrot, scrubbed and sliced
75 g (3 oz) swede, peeled and chopped

1 medium potato, peeled and cut into cubes
300 ml (10 fl oz) water
2 tablespoons Greek yoghurt or creamy fromage frais

Put the chicken and the vegetables into a saucepan and cover with the water. Simmer covered for about 20 minutes or until the vegetables are soft. Purée with some of the cooking liquid and the yoghurt or fromage frais.

makes 6 portions

creamy pink purée

A good way to turn some left-over cooked chicken into a tasty meal for your baby. This is especially good if you add a slice of avocado.

50 g (2 oz) cooked chicken, chopped
50 ml (2 fl oz) milk

1 tomato, peeled, seeded and cut into pieces

Simply blend all the ingredients together to a purée.

makes 2 portions

one-pot chicken with garden vegetables

My daughter Scarlett loved this when she first started to eat chicken and it's very simple to make.

65 g (2½ oz) rice
300 ml (10 fl oz) chicken or vegetable stock (see pages 33–4)
75 g (3 oz) chicken breast, cut into pieces

25 g (1 oz) broccoli florets or peas
25 g (1 oz) carrots, scrubbed and sliced
25 g (1 oz) green beans, chopped
120 ml (4 fl oz) apple juice

Cook the rice in the stock. When the rice is half-cooked, add the chicken, vegetables and pour over the apple juice. Continue to cook until the rice is soft and the vegetables tender, but not overcooked. If necessary, add extra stock to make the purée into a good consistency.

makes 4 portions

liver and apple purée

Liver blends to a lovely smooth consistency, it's very nutritious and cheap to buy and combining it with apple will appeal to your baby.

100 g (4 oz) lamb's or calf's liver
50 ml (2 fl oz) milk

1 apple, peeled, cored and cut into pieces

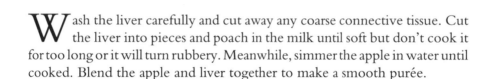

Wash the liver carefully and cut away any coarse connective tissue. Cut the liver into pieces and poach in the milk until soft but don't cook it for too long or it will turn rubbery. Meanwhile, simmer the apple in water until cooked. Blend the apple and liver together to make a smooth purée.

makes 3 portions

beginner's beef casserole

The carrot and swede add a sweetness that babies like. This is an ideal recipe for introducing red meat and it can be puréed to a smooth consistency. This recipe takes a while to cook but it's not labour-intensive.

1 small onion, peeled and sliced
½ small clove garlic, finely chopped (optional)
Margarine or vegetable oil for frying
175 g (6 oz) lean stewing steak, cut into cubes
1 medium carrot, scrubbed and sliced

1 sprig of parsley
300 ml (10 fl oz) beef, chicken or vegetable stock (see pages 33–4)
175 g (6 oz) potato, peeled and cut into cubes
100 g (4 oz) swede, peeled and cut into cubes

Pre-heat the oven to gas mark 4, 350°F (180°C).
Sauté the onion and garlic in the margarine or oil until soft, then add the meat and brown. Put into a small casserole with the carrot and parsley and pour over half the stock. Put in the oven and after 10 minutes turn the temperature down to gas mark 3, 325°F (160°C). After 1 hour, add the potato and swede and pour in the rest of the stock and continue to cook for a further hour. Blend to the desired consistency.

makes 5 portions

melt-in-the-mouth plaice with mushrooms

A great way of adding taste is to flavour the milk in which you cook the fish – in this recipe I have used mace, onion, peppercorns and a bay leaf. You can substitute four peeled, halved, seedless grapes for the button mushrooms as a delicious variation.

A blade of mace
2 peppercorns
1 slice of onion
½ bay leaf
150 ml (5 fl oz) milk
15 g (½ oz) onion, finely chopped
15 g (½ oz) butter or margarine

2 button mushrooms, chopped
1 tablespoon flour
1 × 100-g (4-oz) fillet of plaice, skinned
Knob of butter
Small pinch mixed herbs

Add the mace, peppercorns, onion and bay leaf to the milk and heat without boiling for about 5 minutes. Meanwhile sauté the onion in the butter until soft and then add the chopped mushrooms and cook for a couple of minutes. Stir in the flour, let it cook for a minute and then gradually add the strained milk to make a thick white sauce. Steam or microwave the fish with a little milk, butter or margarine and herbs for 3–4 minutes or until the fish flakes easily with a fork (check carefully for any bones). Mix with the sauce and purée in a blender or mash with a fork.

makes 2 portions

9 TO 12 MONTHS

It is easy to continue making smooth purées and underestimate your baby's ability to chew. However, once your baby has cut a few teeth, vary the texture of the food, try mashing, chopping and grating food – you may be surprised by what a few teeth and strong gums can get through!

At this age, babies are often more interested in the feel than the taste of their food so it is a good idea to have two bowls, one for baby and one for mum. That way you can sneak spoonfuls into her mouth whilst she's busy moisturising her hair with spinach purée! It is also helpful to give your baby lots of soft finger foods. Put a waterproof tablecloth under the high chair (this way you can recycle foods that have mysteriously disappeared) and strew lots of soft, colourful finger foods on the high chair tray. Your baby will really enjoy picking up all the different foods and popping them in his mouth and this will also improve his hand and eye co-ordination.

Once your baby is able to hold toys fairly well, try a cup with a spout. When your baby can manage that, remove the top. This is the messy bit. A cup with a weighted base that doesn't topple over is the best choice and make sure she isn't wearing her best clothes!

Remember never leave your child unattended whilst eating and avoid giving foods that might get stuck in his throat like whole grapes, fruits with stones or nuts. Peanuts are especially dangerous because they are just the right size to block the oesophagus.

IDEAS FOR FINGER FOODS

◆ *steamed vegetables e.g potato, courgettes, cauliflower, broccoli, butternut squash*
◆ *dried fruits*
◆ *grated apple, pear, cucumber or carrot*
◆ *fresh fruits e.g. chunks of banana, or orange segments*
◆ *cooked peas or sweetcorn*
◆ *breakfast cereals like Weetabix or cornflakes mixed with a little milk*

- *grated cheese*
- *miniature sandwiches e.g. mashed banana, cream cheese, or mashed sardines*
- *cooked pasta shapes like little bow-ties or shells*
- *little pieces of cooked chicken or flaked fish*
- *miniature meat or chicken balls*
- *fingers of toast to dip into vegetable purées*
- *rice cakes*

THE QUESTION OF MILK

As I've already explained, it's best to continue with formula milk or breast milk for the first year because it is enriched with vitamins and minerals. However, the good news is that once your baby gets to around 11 months and is crawling around and sticking everything into his mouth there is not much point in sterilizing bottles – just make sure they are washed very thoroughly. Be careful not to let milk sit around in bottles and curdle. Wash them as soon after use as possible. If you have a dishwasher, rinse them out very well and then put them in the machine. Your baby should be able to drink from a cup now, so maybe just offer a bottle at bed-time.

THE CEREAL KILLERS

You can now introduce adult breakfast cereals like Weetabix, porridge, cornflakes, granola and muesli. There is no need to continue with baby cereals which are more expensive, fine textured and tend to be quite bland. However, beware! The once healthy bowl of cereal is looking more and more like a bowl of sweets. Look carefully at the labels, some cereals contain as much as 49 per cent sugar. Choose whole-grain cereals which are low in sugar and salt.

TEETHING

Chewing on something cold and hard can relieve sore gums. Choose something hard so that your baby can't chew off chunks and choke on them and never leave a baby alone with food.

- Trimmed celery stalks
- Chilled scrapped carrots
- Cool chunks of cantaloupe or honeydew melon
- The hard core of a pineapple
- Semi-frozen banana – as this defrosts it will turn into mush in your baby's mouth
- Dried apple rings – your baby can poke her fingers through the hole to hold on to this and you could secure it to the high chair with a piece of string to stop it from falling on the floor
- A piece of bagel
- A rice cake
- Moisten a clean cloth with cold water, wring it out and let your baby chew on it – when Scarlet was nine months old, she

was always chewing on bits of her clothes so this is a good alternative.

◆ You can buy teething rings which are filled with liquid which you can chill in the fridge – don't store a teething ring in the freezer, though, as it will be so cold it could burn your baby's gums.

RUSKS

Manufacturers state that adding sugar to baby foods is undesirable but then they add it to baby rusks. Some rusks contain more sugar than a doughnut. It's simple to make your own sugar-free rusks. Simply cut a thick slice of bread into three strips and bake in an oven pre-heated to gas mark 4, 350°F (180°C) for 15 minutes. You can store these in an airtight container for three or four days. If your child gets frustrated trying to use a spoon you can also prepare fingers of toast and your baby can have fun dipping these into vegetable purées.

stuffed potato

If you are baking potatoes in the oven then why not add an extra one for your baby and make this delicious recipe. Alternatively, simply boil the potato and then mix in the rest of the ingredients.

1 large baking potato (approx. 225 g, 8 oz)
75 g (3 oz) cauliflower or broccoli florets

2 tomatoes, skinned, de-seeded and chopped
25 g (2 oz) Cheddar cheese, grated
A knob of butter
3–4 tablespoons milk

Prick the potato and bake it in the oven. Meanwhile, steam the cauliflower or broccoli until tender. Peel the skin off the potato and mix all the ingredients together with the cooked potato. Process in a blender or mash with a fork.

makes 3 portions

'I don't like vegetables' purée

To encourage babies who are not keen on some vegetables like spinach, mix these with vegetables they do like and top with cheese sauce.

1 medium carrot, scrubbed and sliced
100 g (4 oz) fresh spinach, tough stalks removed
50 g (2 oz) frozen peas
25 g (1 oz) butter

2 tablespoons flour
175 ml (6 fl oz) milk
40 g (1 ½ oz) Cheddar cheese, grated

I cook this is in a multi-layered steamer. Put the sliced carrot in the bottom level of the steamer and cook for 12–15 minutes. Add the spinach and peas on the layer above and continue to cook for about 6 minutes. Melt the butter in a saucepan, add the flour and stir for 1 minute. Add the milk gradually, bring to the boil, reduce the heat and stir until thick and smooth. Stir in the cheese and pour over the vegetables and blend.

makes 3 portions

Popeye purée

Egg yolk and spinach are both rich in iron and you will improve the absorption of the iron in these foods if you give your baby some vitamin C-rich foods at the same meal (e.g. kiwi fruit or orange segments).

225 g (8 oz) fresh or 100 g (4 oz) frozen spinach
25 g (1 oz) butter or margarine
1 tablespoon flour

175 ml (6 fl oz) milk
40 g (1½ oz) Cheddar cheese, grated
A pinch of freshly grated nutmeg
½ hard-boiled egg, finely grated

Remove any tough stalks from the spinach and wash carefully. Cook it, in a little water, until tender. Meanwhile make a white sauce: melt the butter or margarine in a saucepan, stir in the flour and let it cook for 1 minute. Add the milk gradually, stirring over a gentle heat until the sauce thickens and boils. Stir in the cheese and nutmeg. Squeeze any excess water from the spinach, mix with the sauce and purée or chop. Finally add the grated egg.

makes 4 portions

lettuce, cauliflower and courgette purée

This purée tastes so good that I always make a large quantity, I freeze some for my baby and serve the rest as soup for everyone else in the family.

1 onion, peeled and chopped
25 g (1 oz) margarine or 1 tablespoon
sunflower oil
3 courgettes, washed, trimmed and
thinly sliced
225 g (8 oz) cauliflower

225 g (8 oz) crisp lettuce, washed and
shredded
900 ml (1½ pints) chicken or vegetable
stock (see pages 33–4)
300 ml (10 fl oz) extra stock to make a
soup

Sauté the onion in the margarine or oil until soft but not golden. Add the courgettes, cauliflower and lettuce and cook over a low heat for about 4 minutes. Pour over the stock and continue to cook for about 15 minutes over a low heat. Remove about a quarter of the liquid and vegetables and purée in a blender to make the baby's portions. Add the extra stock to the rest and blend to make a delicious smooth soup.

makes 6 baby portions and 4 adult portions

minestrone magic

Babies love fishing out the different ingredients in this soup. Older children love it too, 'Can you catch a green bean?' asks Lara, and Nicholas fishes deep into his bowl with his soup spoon. This game seems to last a long time and second helpings are usually requested to replenish stocks!

1 large onion, peeled and finely sliced
1 garlic clove, crushed
Sunflower oil for frying
2 medium carrots, scrubbed and diced
1 celery stick, diced
2 medium potatoes, peeled and diced, about 275 g (10 oz)
1 × 225 g (8 oz) tin tomatoes, chopped
2.25 litres (4 pints) chicken or vegetable stock (see pages 33–4)

75 g (3 oz) cabbage, shredded
50 g (2 oz) green beans, prepared and cut in half
75 g (3 oz) tiny pasta shapes
50 g (2 oz) frozen peas
1 × 432 g (15 oz) tin of haricot beans
Freshly ground black pepper
25 g (1 oz) freshly grated Parmesan cheese (optional)

Sauté the onion and garlic in the oil until the onions are softened, then add the carrots and celery. Transfer to a large saucepan, add the diced potatoes, tinned tomatoes and their juice and the stock, and simmer for about 20 minutes. Add the cabbage, green beans and pasta and simmer for a further 10 minutes. Finally stir in the frozen peas and the haricot beans and cook for a further 5 minutes. Season with a little freshly ground black pepper and sprinkle over some Parmesan, if you like.

makes 20 portions

mock baked beans

This is a quick and easy home-made version of a popular dish. Beans are a good source of protein and iron. This also makes a good dish for older children.

25 g (1 oz) butter
1 medium onion, peeled and finely chopped
1 ½ tablespoons flour
350 ml (12 fl oz) vegetable stock (see page 34)

2 tablespoons tomato ketchup
1 tablespoon tomato purée
1 teaspoon soft brown sugar
1 x 400-g (14-oz) tin white kidney beans

Melt the butter in a frying pan and sauté the onion until soft and lightly golden. Add the flour and cook over a gentle heat for 1 minute. Gradually stir in the vegetable stock. Bring to the boil, then reduce the heat and simmer for 2 to 3 minutes until thickened and smooth. Stir in the tomato ketchup, tomato purée and sugar and cook for 2 minutes. Drain the kidney beans and add these to the sauce, bring to the boil and then simmer for about 2 minutes. For babies either mash with a fork or purée in a blender. For some babies you may wish to purée these in a mouli which will get rid of the outer skin of the kidney beans, which can be difficult to digest.

makes 8 portions

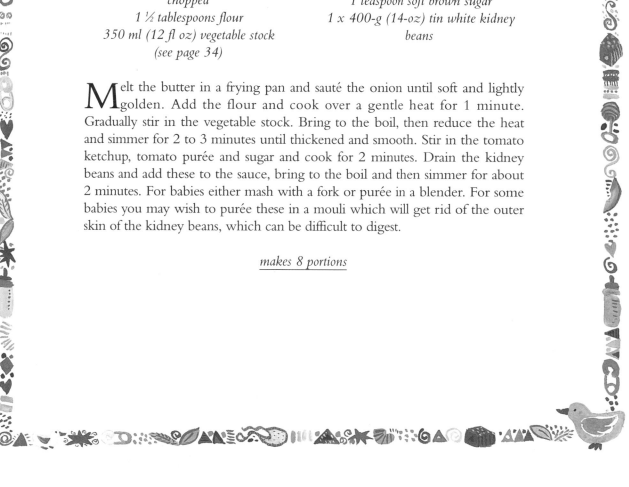

creamy fish with tomatoes

Cooking fish in parcels of greaseproof paper or foil seals in the flavour and saves on washing-up! I use greaseproof paper when cooking in a microwave and foil when cooking in the oven. Probably the best fish for young babies is plaice or hake because it is very soft and purées well. For older babies who can cope with more lumpy food then try using haddock or cod. In the following recipe you could use other vegetables like carrots, leeks and courgettes instead of the tomatoes. Try a sprinkling of chopped fresh herbs too.

½ small onion, peeled and chopped
15 g (½ oz) butter or margarine and extra for dotting
2 tomatoes, peeled, de-seeded and cut into pieces
1 bay leaf

3 tablespoons double cream or fromage frais
25g (1 oz) Edam or Cheddar cheese, grated (optional)
100 g (4 oz) skinned fillet of plaice or sole

Sauté the onion in the butter or margarine until soft, then add the tomatoes and bay leaf. Cook them for a couple of minutes and then stir in the cream or fromage frais. Cut the foil or greaseproof paper into a circle large enough to cover the fish. Place the fish on the foil or paper, dot with a little butter, spoon over the onion and tomato mixture, removing the bay leaf, and sprinkle with cheese. Then fold the circle in half and roll the edges together to form a parcel.

Cook in a microwave on full power for 3 to 4 minutes or cook in the oven (at gas mark 4, 350°F, 180°C) wrapped in foil for 15 to 20 minutes. Pick out any bones, then purée or chop in a blender, adding a little milk to make into a smooth purée if necessary.

makes 3 portions

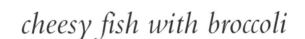

cheesy fish with broccoli

This makes a good first fish recipe and it is best to put it through a mouli for young babies. Not only is broccoli a rich source of vitamins A and C, but recent studies in America show evidence that eating broccoli may help to protect us against certain forms of cancer.

100–175 g (4–6 oz) fillet of plaice
1 slice of peeled onion
sprig of parsley or bay leaf
200 ml (7 fl oz) milk
75 g (3 oz) broccoli, cut into florets

15 g (½ oz) butter or margarine
1 tablespoon flour
40 g (1½ oz) Cheddar, Emmenthal or
Gruyère cheese, grated

Put the fish fillet into an ovenproof dish, together with the onion and parsley or bay leaf and pour over 50 ml (2 fl oz) of the milk. Cover and cook in the oven (at gas mark 4, 350°F, 180°C) for about 12 minutes or in the microwave on high for about 3 minutes. The fish will flake easily with a fork when cooked. Meanwhile steam the broccoli for about 5 minutes.

Once the fish is cooked, strain the cooking liquid and flake the fish carefully to make sure there are no bones and set aside. Melt the butter or margarine and stir in the flour. Cook for 30 seconds, then gradually stir in the remaining milk to make a smooth sauce. Stir in the grated cheese and add the cooked broccoli and flaked fish. Blend or mouli to the required consistency.

makes 3 portions

pasta primavera

This is popular with my whole family and you can prepare the sauce in advance and freeze it in small containers to be used at your convenience. If your child is a confirmed non-vegetable eater, resort to disguise and purée the sauce. The type of pasta you use will depend on your baby's eating skills!

2 tablespoons olive oil
1 small onion, peeled and finely chopped
1 small clove garlic, finely choppped
½ red or yellow pepper, de-seeded and finely chopped
2 medium courgettes, topped, tailed and diced
100 g (4 oz) mushrooms, sliced (optional)

225 g (8 oz) fresh tomatoes skinned, de-seeded and chopped or 1 × 800-g (1 lb 12 oz) tin chopped tomatoes, drained
1 tablespoon tomato purée
1 tablespoon milk
A little dried basil or oregano (optional)
100 g (4 oz) pasta
A little grated Parmesan cheese (optional)

Sauté the onion and garlic in the olive oil for about 4 minutes, then add the chopped pepper and continue to cook for 3 to 4 minutes. Add the remaining ingredients, except the pasta and Parmesan, and simmer for about 15 minutes. Meanwhile, cook the pasta in boiling water until tender. Drain the pasta and mix with the sauce when it is ready. Sprinkle over Parmesan to serve if you wish.

makes 5 portions

Lara's tomato and cheese pasta sauce

If your baby or toddler is a pasta groupie, like my daughter Lara, then this sauce is a great way to make sure she's getting a good supply of calcium – so important for healthy bones and teeth. Serve with freshly cooked pasta.

1 medium onion, peeled and finely sliced
1 tablespoon vegetable oil
1 x 400 g (14 oz) tin tomatoes, chopped
1 tablespoon tomato purée

¼ teaspoon mixed herbs
¼ teaspoon oregano
Freshly ground black pepper
75 g (3 oz) Cheddar cheese
50 g (2 oz) Mozzarella cheese, grated

Gently sauté the onion in the oil in a covered pan, stirring occasionally for 10 minutes until softened but not browned. Stir in the tomatoes, tomato purée, herbs and pepper and simmer for 10 minutes. Remove from the heat and mix in the cheese until melted. Liquidize in a blender and serve the sauce over pasta.

makes 8 portions of sauce

tasty liver strips

This recipe for liver makes good finger food and it's nice and soft for your baby to chew.

175 g (6 oz) calf's liver, trimmed and cut into strips
1 tablespoon flour
Vegetable oil for frying
½ onion, peeled and chopped

50 g (2 oz) button mushrooms, sliced
1 dessertspoon tomato purée
175 ml (6 fl oz) beef, chicken or vegetable stock (see pages 33–4)

Toss the liver in the flour and brown it in the oil. Don't cook it for long or it will become tough. Remove and set aside. Meanwhile, in the same pan, sauté the onion until soft, then add the mushrooms and cook for 2 minutes. Add the tomato purée, stock and the liver strips and simmer for 10 to 15 minutes. Serve as finger food, chop or purée.

makes 6 portions

my first shepherd's pie

This is one of the best recipes for introducing your baby to red meat. The potato gives it a creamy texture and the vegetables add lots of flavour.

750 g (1½ lb) potatoes, peeled and cut into chunks
25 g (1 oz) butter or margarine
3 tablespoons milk
½ onion, peeled and chopped
½ celery stick, chopped

1 medium carrot, chopped
Vegetable oil for frying
100 g (4 oz) lean minced meat
100 g (4 oz) tinned tomatoes, chopped
120 ml (4 fl oz) chicken stock

Boil the potatoes until tender, then mash them together with the butter and milk. Meanwhile sauté the onion, celery and carrot in vegetable oil for about 10 minutes or until softened. Brown the meat in some more vegetable oil and then chop in a food processor to make it softer for your baby to chew. Mix the chopped meat with the tomatoes and sautéed vegetables, pour over the stock and simmer for about 20 minutes. Mix the meat mixture together with the mashed potatoes and chop in a food processor to make it super smooth.

makes 7 portions

my first spaghetti bolognese

A good way to encourage your baby to eat meat is to make a tasty pasta sauce. I cook the pasta until it is nice and soft and I chop the meat to make it very smooth. Scarlett, my one-year-old daughter, loves sucking spaghetti into her mouth and has as much fun playing with it as eating it!

50 g (2 oz) spaghetti
25 g (1 oz) chopped onion
½ red pepper, de-seeded and chopped
Vegetable oil for frying
100 g (4 oz) lean minced beef

½ teaspoon tomato purée
2 medium tomatoes, skinned, de-seeded and chopped
120 ml (4 fl oz) chicken or vegetable stock (see pages 33–4)

Cook the pasta and cut it up into pieces. Meanwhile, sauté the onion and pepper in the oil until soft. Add the meat and brown it, then add the tomato purée, chopped tomatoes and stock and simmer for about 10 minutes. Chop the meat in a food processor and pour this sauce over the pasta.

makes 3 portions

risotto with chicken liver

This is another way of dressing up liver to appeal to children.

50 g (2 oz) whole-grain rice
1 small onion, peeled and chopped
½ small red pepper, de-seeded and
chopped
Vegetable oil for frying
50 g (2 oz) chicken liver, cut into pieces

50 ml (2 fl oz) chicken or vegetable
stock (see pages 33–4)
50 ml (2 fl oz) apple juice
40 g (1½ oz) frozen peas
1 hard-boiled egg, chopped into pieces

Cook the rice. Meanwhile, sauté the onion and pepper in a little oil until soft, then add the liver and sauté for about 1 minute. Pour over the stock and apple juice, add the frozen peas and simmer for 4 to 5 minutes. Chop the cooked liver into pieces and add this together with the rest of the peas and pepper mixture to the cooked rice. Finally add the chopped hard-boiled egg.

makes 2 portions

creamy fruit with tofu

Soft tofu has a creamy texture that is appealing to babies and combining
dried fruit with tofu takes away its intense sweetness.

65 g (2½ oz) mixed dried fruit　　*2 tablespoons creamy natural yoghurt*
75 g (3 oz) soft tofu

Cover the fruit with water and simmer for about 10 minutes or until soft.
Blend together with the tofu and yoghurt.

makes 4 portions

mixed fruit compote

Dried fruits tend to have a laxative effect on babies so I like to mix fresh
and dried fruits together. This purée is good mixed with milk and baby
rice, natural fromage frais, yoghurt or sieved cottage cheese.

100 g (4 oz) mixed dried fruit　　*2 apples, peeled, cored and cut into*
1 short cinnamon stick (optional)　　　　　　*pieces*
　　　　　　　　　　　　2 pears, peeled, cored and cut into pieces

Put the dried fruit into a saucepan and cover with water (add the cinnamon
stick if you like). Simmer the fruit for about 10 minutes then add the fresh
fruit and cook for a further 4 minutes. Discard the cinnamon stick and blend
the cooked fruit to the desired consistency.

makes 6 portions

creamy apple dessert

You should be giving more grated and chopped food now. This will take only a couple of minutes to prepare. The lemon juice is to stop the apple turning brown.

1 apple, peeled, cored and grated
Squeeze of lemon juice (optional)
4 chopped raisins
1 small pot fromage frais or

2 tablespoons Greek yoghurt
1 tablespoon apple juice
Pinch of cinnamon (optional)

Simply combine all the the ingredients together.

makes 2 portions

TODDLERS

MOVING ON

'That's yucky! I'm not eating it' – these words are guaranteed to cut close to any parent's heart and you are a very lucky mother indeed if your toddler enjoys eating and you have never experienced stubbornness, lack of interest or unreasonable fussiness when it comes to mealtimes. So many parents find that at around the age of one their child suddenly changes from being a good eater, enthusiastically anticipating the treats in store as he sits strapped into his high chair, to going on virtual hunger strike. Life is too exciting to worry about food when you've just learned to walk and threatening your two-year-old that he won't grow up 'big and strong like Daddy' and doing your version of the can-can on the kitchen table will do little to encourage him to eat his plate of sardines.

After the age of one, a child's weight gain slows down dramatically. Whereas a child might gain 9 kg (20 lbs) in his first year, it is quite normal to gain only 1.8 or 2.2 (4 or 5) in his second. You'll notice how his chubby baby body slims down as he becomes more active. Health bears little relationship to weight gain and a child's energy level and zest for life are a much better guide. Making a big deal about your child's eating (or not eating) will only steel his resolve.

Most toddlers are just beginning to assert their new-found independence and enjoy bringing their poor parents to the brink of despair in a tough battle of wills. Just when you think you have won and your two-year-old has condescended to pick up a wafer-thin slice of apple that has been sitting on his plate for the last 20 minutes, he suddenly discovers a microscopic blemish on the fruit. In his own inimitable, finicky way, he hurls it on the floor in such a disdainful manner as if to say 'you can't really expect me to eat *that*'.

Eventually your child wears you down to such an extent that you can't face cooking for him any more. You no longer care what he eats as long as he eats something. Out come the crisps and as you turn your back to open the freezer door and reach for the ice-cream, he knows that he has won.

Don't despair, some of the following lines of action will help.

◆ *DON'T GIVE IN!*: You can relax in the knowledge that no child has ever willingly starved himself to death. If your child won't eat his meal, call a halt to the proceedings. Leave some good wholesome food within his reach and when he is hungry he will eat without any coaxing on your part.

◆ *PEER PRESSURE*: Go to a friend's house for tea where there is a child who likes 'tucking in' and you may find that your child will eat whatever is offered.

◆ *'HELPING' IN THE KITCHEN*: One of the best ways to encourage children to eat is to involve them in preparing the meal. Children are more likely to taste dishes they've helped to make. Even helping to unload the shopping often arouses curiosity to try new foods.

◆ *VARYING THE VENUE*: You can work wonders by transporting stubborn eaters to the garden, or simply lay out a picnic on the kitchen floor.

◆ *GIVE AND TAKE*: One of the commonest reasons for fights about food is that children use them to assert their independence. Try negotiating and offer your child a choice – give her three vegetables and let her choose which two she eats.

◆ *LOOKING AND SOUNDING GOOD*: Why not spend a few minutes arranging the food on your child's plate in such a way as to capture his roving eye. (See Fish-shaped salmon cakes or Funny face burgers on pages 87 and 188) Or make your child a mini portion of his own like a shepherd's pie in a ramekin dish.

Giving dishes names helps too – Goldilocks' Porridge, Mermaid Morsels, Thomas The Tank Engine Minestrone – your four-year-old will be impressed if he thinks he is eating his cartoon character's favourite food.

◆ *EATING WITH YOUR CHILD*: It is a good idea to eat with your child and mealtimes should be enjoyed but there must be a difference between playing and eating. You may be quite happy for a while to play aeroplanes with fork loads of shepherd's pie and name individual sardines after the characters in *Sesame Street* but making a game out of eating may make your child dependent on Mum's personalized service long after your patience has been stretched to its limit. Children are great mimics so if they see you 'tucking-in' . . .

◆ *COMBINING FOODS*: Try mixing new foods with old favourites. Adding fruit often makes food more appealing (like my recipe for Chicken balls with apples and courgettes on page 119).

◆ *FOREIGN FOODS*: Many foreign foods are

made with healthy ingredients – take a stir-fry, for example, which is full of lovely crisp vegetables. There are some delicious ethnic recipes in this book which are simple to make, like the Indonesian rice dish Nasi goreng (see page 96). To encourage your child to be more adventurous, next time he has his friends over for a meal lay out a taste table with a selection of unusual foods like chicken yakitori, taramasalata, hummus, satay, and exotic fruits.

◆ *FAST FOOD*: Not all convenience food is bad for children. In the 'Healthy junk food' chapter, I have designed recipes which use many of the foods we regularly stock in our larder to make delicious simple meals which will appeal to your toddler's fast food inclinations.

EATING OUT

Why is it that when children go to a restaurant they are offered such a limited choice of foods so ill-suited to the needs of their growing bodies? Have you ever seen a children's menu that did not offer sausages and chips followed by synthetic ice-cream and a squidge of sickly sweet sauce? Ask any restaurateur and he'll say it's because that's the food that children like. It's a vicious circle. Children get used to these over-processed, fatty, artificially flavoured and highly coloured foods and refuse to eat or even try more natural foods. Parents would be much better off ordering something simple from the main menu like a pasta dish and letting their child eat some of their food. Mum or Dad's meal is always more enticing anyway and one thing's guaranteed – the more you say 'No, you can't have any of mine' the more they'll want some!

HEALTHY SNACKS

Adults are conditioned into eating three meals a day whether they are hungry or not. Toddlers have more sense and no amount of coaxing will get them to eat when they don't feel like it. I have included plenty of ideas for healthy snacks because many young children get most of their nutrition from the food they eat between meals. Limiting snacks to fruit and raw vegetables and cutting out sweet fruit juices will soon encourage a healthy appetite at mealtimes.

EASY ON THE SALT

When cooking for children, go easy on the salt and never add salt at the table. Whenever possible, use herbs and spices for flavouring instead. Research has shown that a high salt intake can result in high blood pressure and hypertension in adult life.

BRING ON THE BREAKFAST

Breakfast is big business for cereal manufacturers. In Great Britain alone, over £700 million pounds are spent a year on our children's breakfasts. We are told that children who eat a good breakfast perform better at school and although it can sometimes turn into a battle of wills, we all try to send our children to school with some good nourishing food inside them. However, as far as cereal manufacturers are concerned, there is a conflict between healthy diets and healthy profits. Healthy cereals like Shreddies or Weetabix contain only minimal amounts of sugar, whereas many of the latest 'designer' cereals can contain as much as 49 per cent sugar. The once healthy bowl of cereal is looking more and more like a bowl of sweets.

These refined cereals are so lacking in nutrients that there need to be long lists of vitamins and minerals added to replace all the goodness lost in the processing. Many mothers reading the long lists of nutritional information on the packets are persuaded to believe that these sugary, vitamin-enriched cereals are good for their children and children get used to the colourful packets, novelty gifts and sweet-tasting cereals and come to regard these as real food refusing anything else on offer.

There are many nutritious grains which can be mixed together to make your own delicious recipes. Wheatgerm is particularly good and can be sprinkled onto natural yoghurt mixed with some fresh fruit and a little honey. It is easy to make wonderful home-made mueslis combining rolled oats and wheatgerm with fresh and dried fruits, coconut and some grated or chopped nuts. This can be mixed with milk, yoghurt or fruit juice and sweetened with a little honey if necessary. I've included two of my favourite recipes here but there are endless variations on this theme using whichever fruits happen to be in season. If we can encourage our children to enjoy eating healthy wholegrain cereals from an early age, then hopefully they will reject these sickly, sweet cereals which manufacturers produce, especially for children.

Cereals aren't the end of the story either. With a little imagination your child can enjoy a variety of delicious, healthy breakfasts that will set him up for the day ahead.

HANDY TIPS FOR BETTER BREAKFASTS

◆ Muffins are great for breakfast and you can bake lots of delicious healthy foods inside them. Cook them the day before or you can freeze a batch and take one or two out the night before. (See pages 74, 128, 135 for muffin recipes.)

◆ If your child is a bad eater but tends to be most hungry at breakfast time, give him a cooked breakfast like a vegetable omelette or maybe even offer something from last night's dinner.

◆ Add fresh fruit to shop-bought breakfast cereals and let your child make his own combinations. Nicholas makes his own 'muesli' by mixing Cornflakes, crushed Weetabix, Shreddies, raisins and sliced banana.

◆ Sealed toasted sandwiches made in an electric sandwich maker are delicious. Try cheese and tomato or ham and cheese. Take extra care as fillings stay very hot.

◆ If your child doesn't like drinking milk, try hot chocolate or, for lovers of peanut butter, 2–3 tablespoons or drinking chocolate mixed with 175 ml (6 fl oz) hot milk and blended with a banana and a spoonful of peanut butter **N**. For a treat, use cold milk and add a scoop of chocolate ice-cream. Also try delicious milkshakes: 1–2 large stoned dates, 1 banana and 120 ml (4 fl oz) milk blended together; a small carton raspberry yoghurt, 1 small banana and 120 ml (4 fl oz) chilled milk; or use raspberries and strawberries, or any favourite tinned fruit in natural juice to blend with the milk.

◆ Always try to get your child to eat fresh fruit for breakfast – try different varieties and, if you have time, cut them into interesting shapes and arrange them in a pattern on the plate as this always makes it more enticing.

◆ Buy some miniature, coloured carrier bags and fill them with a mixture of healthy cereals – you could even put a little free gift at the bottom of the bag so that your child has to eat up all his cereal before he can get it!

◆ Make a warming bowl of porridge and add chopped fresh fruit to it or even peanut butter and raisins **N**.

◆ Cooked dried fruit mixed with fresh fruit and served with yoghurt and fromage frais can be sprinkled with cereals to make a complete breakfast.

◆ Make scrambled eggs more exciting by

mixing in cheese and sautéed tomatoes and spring onions.

◈ French toast, sliced bread dipped in a mixture of beaten egg and milk and fried in butter, is delicious for breakfast, particularly if you make it with raisin bread. As breakfast is often a bit of a rush, you can make several portions in advance, store it in the fridge or freezer, and then re-heat in a toaster.

rich fruity muesli ✳

This is the type of breakfast to set you up for a day's skiing on a mountain in Switzerland. It's quite delicious and can be prepared the night before if necessary. You can add lots of different fruits like strawberries or peaches if you wish.

75 g (3 oz) rolled oats
40 g (1½ oz) toasted wheatgerm
250 ml (8 fl oz) apple juice
2 teaspoons lemon juice
1 large apple, peeled and grated
1 small orange, cut into segments with the pith removed
6 grapes (preferably black), halved and seeded

1 small banana, peeled and sliced
1 heaped tablespoon raisins
2 tablespoons finely chopped hazelnuts (optional)
2 tablespoons Greek or vanilla yoghurt
2 tablespoons double cream (optional)
2 teaspoons honey

Soak the oats and wheatgerm in the apple juice for about 30 minutes or overnight. Sprinkle the lemon juice over the grated apple and then simply combine all the ingredients together. Decorate with fruit.

makes 3 portions

blissful banana bread N

Lovely and moist. Serve plain or buttered – great for breakfast or lunch-boxes. This is a favourite with my family.

100g (4 oz) butter or margarine
100 g (4 oz) brown sugar
1 egg
450 g (1 lb) bananas, mashed
3 tablespoons Greek yoghurt
1 teaspoon vanilla essence
250 g (8 oz) plain flour

1 tablespoon baking powder
1 teaspoon ground cinnamon
Pinch of salt
90 g (3 1/2 oz) raisins
65 g (2 1/2 oz) chopped pecans or walnuts

Pre-heat the oven to gas mark 4, 350°F (180°C) and grease a 2-lb (900-g) loaf tin.

Beat the butter or margarine and sugar together until creamy then add the egg and continue to beat until smooth. Add the mashed bananas, yoghurt and vanilla essence. Sift together the flour, baking powder, cinnamon and salt and beat this gradually into the banana mixture. Finally stir in the raisins and chopped nuts. Bake for about 1 hour to 1 hour 15 minutes or until a cocktail stick inserted in the centre comes out clean.

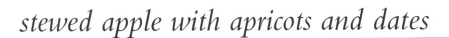

stewed apple with apricots and dates

Adding dried fruit to cooking apples is a way of sweetening them without using sugar. This fruit trio has a wonderful flavour and it is delicious for breakfast as well as after a meal. Serve plain or with fromage frais, yoghurt or custard.

1 large cooking apple
3 large dates
4 dried apricots

6 tablespoons apple juice
4 tablespoons water

Peel, core and chop the apple. Peel off the outer skin of the dates and remove the stones. Chop the dates and apricots. Put the fruit into a saucepan together with the apple juice and water, and simmer for 15 to 20 minutes or until the apples are soft and mushy.

makes 2 portions

VEGETABLE VARIETY

You don't need to be a vegetarian to enjoy vegetable dishes as a main meal. There are lots of delicious recipes to choose from in this section which will encourage your child to like vegetables. You can also adapt some of the recipes in the Baby section – Cinderella's pumpkin (see page 36) and Lettuce, cauliflower and courgette purée (see page 47) make wonderful soups and Mock baked beans (see page 49) are a particular favourite with my baby daughter Scarlett and my husband Simon! A selection of raw or steamed vegetables served with a dipping sauce decorated to look like an animal's face is great for birthday parties and can be more intriguing than a plate of crisps (see page 129).

Vegetable pasta salads are very popular with children, they love to pick out all the different coloured vegetables and pasta shapes and they are quick to prepare and look very attractive. Stuffed baked potatoes are another favourite – these can be packed with lots of healthy ingredients and are very easy to make. Vegetable quiches can be cut into individual portions and frozen ready to be used at your convenience. Beans and lentils are cheap and you can use them in salads, soups and stews.

The shorter the storage time and the cooler the conditions in which vegetables are kept, the fresher the vegetables and the more nutrients they contain. If possible it is better to shop more often for fresh produce rather than buying in bulk and keeping it lingering in your larder. Interestingly, commercially frozen food in the UK is frozen so soon after it is picked that sometimes frozen food can be 'fresher' than fresh produce on the shelves. Try to keep all fruit and vegetables loosely wrapped in the fridge (although bananas should be stored in a cool larder) and use as soon as possible.

As the table overleaf shows, frozen vegetables which are not overcooked can be almost as nutritious as fresh vegetables. However, tinned peas after cooking have lost most of their vitamin C. The best

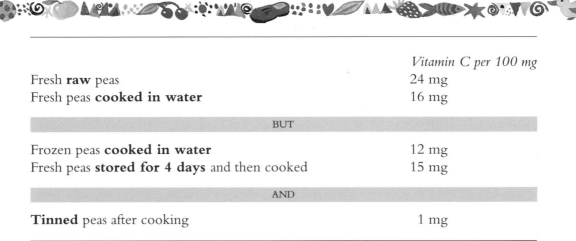

	Vitamin C per 100 mg
Fresh **raw** peas	24 mg
Fresh peas **cooked in water**	16 mg
BUT	
Frozen peas **cooked in water**	12 mg
Fresh peas **stored for 4 days** and then cooked	15 mg
AND	
Tinned peas after cooking	1 mg

method of cooking to retain as many nutrients as possible is steaming or microwaving. Boiled broccoli retains only 35 per cent of its vitamin C as opposed to 72 per cent when it is steamed or microwaved. Scrub or wash fruit and vegetables rather than peeling them as most of the vitamins lie just beneath the surface. Also, it is much better to boil vegetables whole whenever possible, they may cook faster if cut into small pieces, but vitamin loss increases the more you divide them.

floating mushroom soup

My daughter Lara loves mushrooms and rice and so I have combined them together to make this recipe. I prefer to use flat mushrooms rather than button mushrooms as they have a better flavour.

225 g (8 oz) flat mushrooms
1 onion, peeled and chopped
40 g (1½ oz) butter or margarine
25 g (1 oz) flour
1.2 litres (2 pints) chicken or vegetable stock (see pages 33–4)

1 tablespoon whole-grain rice
1 bay leaf
Salt and freshly ground pepper
2 tablespoons cream or fromage frais
1 heaped tablespoon chopped fresh chives

Wash the mushrooms, wipe them dry and thinly slice them. Sauté the onion in the butter or margarine until soft, then add the mushrooms. Cover the mushrooms with some greaseproof paper and put a lid over the frying pan. Simmer for about 5 minutes. Stir in the flour and pour over the stock. Add the rice and bay leaf, bring to the boil and simmer for about 20 minutes. Season with a little salt and pepper and stir in the cream or fromage frais and chives. Remove the bay leaf before serving.

makes 6 portions

tasty tomato soup

There's somthing very homely and comforting about a delicious bowl of tomato soup. It's also easy to turn it into a complete meal by adding some cooked rice and diced chicken.

1 medium onion, peeled and sliced
1 medium carrot, about 50 g (2 oz), washed, scrubbed and sliced
25 g (1 oz) butter
25 g (1 oz) plain flour
350 g (12 oz) fresh tomatoes, skinned, de-seeded and sliced
1 x 400-g (14-oz) tin tomatoes, drained and chopped

600 ml (1 pint) chicken or vegetable stock (see pages 33–4)
1 bay leaf
1 teaspoon sugar
A little salt and freshly ground black pepper
4 tablespoons evaporated milk or cream

Sauté the onion and carrot in butter until soft (about 6 minutes). Stir in the flour, then add the tomatoes, stock, bay leaf, sugar and seasoning. Bring to the boil and simmer for 20 to 30 minutes. Remove the bay leaf and blend the soup until smooth in a food processor. Finally stir in the evaporated milk or cream and serve.

makes 5 portions

onion soup with floating stars

The secret of a good onion soup is long, slow cooking of the onions which brings out the delicious sweet flavour that children love. The floating stars on top make this soup irresistible! I prefer to use potato rather than flour to thicken the soup.

450 g (1 lb) onions, peeled and finely sliced
1 clove garlic, finely chopped
25 g (1 oz) butter
1 tablespoon olive oil
½ teaspoon granulated sugar
1.2 litres (2 pints) chicken or vegetable

stock (see pages 33–4)
1 large potato, peeled and cubed
6 slices of bread
Butter or margarine for spreading
6 slices of Gruyère cheese
A little freshly ground black pepper

Melt the butter together with the olive oil in a large casserole. Then sauté the onions together with the garlic and sprinkle with the sugar. Cover and cook gently for 30 to 40 minutes letting the onions stew in their own juices until soft. Remove the lid, turn up the heat, and cook the onions, stirring occasionally, until lightly browned. Meanwhile put the stock into a saucepan with the potato and simmer for about 10 minutes or until the potato is soft. Blend the potato and chicken stock in a liquidizer.

Pour the thickened chicken stock over the onions and simmer gently, uncovered, for 20–30 minutes. To finish off, spread some bread with butter or margarine and put a slice of the Gruyère cheese on top. Cut out shapes with a star-shaped biscuit cutter and put these under the grill until the cheese has melted. Season and place a star on the top of each bowl of soup. (You can also add a teaspoon of grated cheese to each bowl of soup.)

makes 6 portions

chopped cobb salad ✳

We spent a magical Christmas holiday in Disneyworld Florida. This salad recipe is the speciality at The Brown Derby Restaurant in the MGM studio complex where we ate on several occasions. Traditionally, the salad is made with blue cheese and bacon. I have removed the bacon from my recipe because it's very fatty and you could substitute a different cheese, for example, Gruyère, in place of the blue cheese if your child prefers it. The meat is also optional. The chopped avocado should not be added to the salad until just before it is served or it will turn brown.

1 hard-boiled egg
25 g (1 oz) Roquefort cheese
90 g (3½ oz) iceberg lettuce
75 g (3 oz) cooked turkey or chicken breast (optional)
1 tablespoon balsamic or red wine vinegar

2 tablespoons olive oil
Pinch of sugar
1 tablespoon snipped chives or chopped spring onion
Salt and freshly ground black pepper
½ avocado, stoned and the flesh scooped out

Finely chop the egg, Roquefort, lettuce and turkey or chicken (if using) and put into a bowl. Prepare the dressing by whisking the vinegar into the oil, followed by the sugar and chives or spring onion. Season lightly. Just before eating chop the avocado flesh and add to the ingredients in the bowl before pouring over the dressing.

makes 3 portions

creamy potato parcels

Stuffed potatoes make a delicious meal served with a salad or perhaps raw
vegetables and a dip (see pages 129–31).

2 large potatoes
Oil for brushing
Salt
*2 tablespoons soft cream cheese or
fromage frais*
50 g (2 oz) Mozzarella cheese, grated
25 g (1 oz) Parmesan cheese, grated

25 g (1 oz) Cheddar cheese, grated
*1 tomato, skinned, de-seeded and
chopped*
2 spring onions, finely chopped
Salt and freshly ground black pepper
*A little extra grated Cheddar cheese for
sprinkling*

Pre-heat the oven to gas mark 6, 400°F (200°C). Prick the skin of the
potatoes and brush them with oil and sprinkle with a little salt. Bake for
1¼ hours or until soft. Halve the potatoes lengthways, scoop out the flesh into
a bowl and mash together with the cheeses, tomato, spring onions and
seasoning.

Spoon the mixture back into the potato shells and sprinkle with the extra
grated Cheddar cheese. Bake for another 10 to 15 minutes or until golden.

makes 4 portions

delicious vegetable rissoles

I make fresh breadcrumbs for this recipe by putting 2 slices
of wholemeal bread in a food processor.

2 medium carrots (about 150 g, 5 oz),
grated
100 g (4 oz) butternut squash, grated
75 g (3 oz) white of leek, finely chopped
100 g (4 oz) button mushrooms, finely
chopped

1 tablespoon parsley
100 g (4 oz) wholemeal breadcrumbs
2 teaspoons soy sauce
1 egg, lightly beaten
Salt and freshly ground black pepper
Vegetable oil for frying

Sauté the leek for 2 minutes and squeeze some of the juices from the grated carrots and squash. Mix with the other vegetables, parsley, breadcrumbs, soy sauce, beaten egg and seasoning and chop for a few seconds in a food processor. Using your hands, form into about 12 rissoles. Heat the oil in a large frying pan and sauté the rissoles over a medium heat for about 8 to 10 minutes, turning occasionally until golden and cooked through.

<u>*makes 12 rissoles*</u>

rice is nice

50 g (2 oz) brown rice
2 eggs, separated
15 g (^{1}/$_2$ oz) melted butter or margarine
175 ml (6 fl oz) milk

100 g (4 oz) Gruyère cheese, grated
Salt and freshly ground black pepper
2 medium tomatoes, sliced
1 heaped tablespoon Parmesan, grated

Pre-heat the oven to gas mark 4, 350°F (180°C). Cook the rice according to the instructions on the packet. Beat the egg yolks and mix with butter or margarine, milk and Gruyère cheese. Season and stir into the cooked rice. Beat the egg whites until stiff and fold them into the egg and rice mixture. Pour into a greased glass ovenproof dish and top with the sliced tomatoes. Sprinkle over the Parmesan and bake for about 35 minutes.

<u>*makes 3 portions*</u>

sesame tofu fingers ❋

Tofu can taste very bland but left to soak in this marinade it takes on a delicious flavour. A crisp sesame seed coating on the outside combines well with the soft tofu. Don't be alarmed at the use of the sake and honey – most of the marinade won't actually be eaten and, anyway, the alcohol is evaporated during cooking! These make a delicious meal served with noodles and stir-fried vegetables.

1 × 10½-oz (297-g) box of firm tofu　　*¼ small onion, peeled and chopped*
2 tablespoons soy sauce　　*Wholewheat flour for coating*
2 tablespoons sake or dry sherry　　*Sesame seeds for coating*
(optional)　　*Vegetable oil for frying*
1 tablespoon honey

Carefully drain the liquid from the tofu and cut into domino-shaped pieces. Combine the soy sauce, sake or sherry (if using), honey and onion and marinate the tofu in the mixture overnight or for at least 2 hours. When you are ready to eat coat the tofu in a mixture of flour and sesame seeds and fry in hot oil until browned (about 4 minutes). They can be eaten hot or cold.

makes 3 portions

cheese, onion and tomato tart

This is a delicious tart and can be served hot or cold. It can be frozen in individual portions for your child and re-heated in the oven. It's a good addition to your child's lunch-box. If you prefer, use frozen wholemeal pastry instead of making your own (you'll need 150 g, 5 oz).

100 g (4 oz) wholemeal flour
1 teaspoon baking powder
100 g (4 oz) butter or margarine
25 g (1 oz) finely grated Parmesan
cheese
A pinch of dry mustard
A pinch of salt
½ beaten egg
2 tablespoons cold water

3 onions, peeled and sliced
3 eggs
3 tablespoons milk or cream
A little freshly grated nutmeg
Salt and freshly ground black pepper
175 g (6 oz) mature Cheddar cheese,
grated
4 medium tomatoes, washed and thinly
sliced

To make the pastry, put the flour and baking powder in a bowl and rub in 50 g (2 oz) of the butter or margarine until the mixture resembles crumbs. Add the Parmesan, mustard powder and salt. Make a well in the centre, add the beaten egg and water and knead to make a firm dough. Wrap in cling film and put in the fridge for at least 30 minutes.

Pre-heat the oven to gas mark 6, 400°F (200°C). Roll out the pastry on a lightly floured board and line a greased, 20-cm (8-inch) flan tin. Prick the base all over with a fork, line with greaseproof paper, fill with baking beans and bake blind (i.e. without the filling) for about 10 minutes.

Meanwhile to prepare the filling, fry the onions in the remaining butter or margarine over a low heat until soft but not browned. Beat the eggs together with the milk or cream, add a little nutmeg and season lightly with salt and pepper. Stir in the Cheddar cheese.

Lay the onions over the base of the flan, pour over the cheese mixture and arrange the sliced tomatoes on top. Bake for 30 minutes at gas mark 6, 400°F (200°C) or until the filling has set.

makes 6 portions

tasty tofu and peanut butter stir-fry

Tofu or beancurd is high in proetin and low in fat. It is very versatile and soft to chew. Thre are two types of tofu, one is very soft (called 'silken') and the other more solid. This tasty recipe goes down very well with my kids and adults love it too!

2 tablespoons dark soy sauce
2 tablespoons smooth peanut butter
1 teaspoon brown sugar
50 g (2 oz) thin egg noodles
4 tablespoons sesame or sunflower oil
1 x 279 g pack firm beancurd, cut into
1-cm (1/2-inch) cubes and rolled in flour
6 spring onions, finely sliced
75 g (3 oz) Chinese cabbage, washed
and shredded
175 g (6 oz) bean sprouts

Mix together the soy sauce, peanut butter and sugar. Cook the noodles according to the directions on the packet and set aside. In a wok or frying pan heat 3 tablespoons of the oil, and fry the cubes of beancurd until golden brown on all sides (about 5 mintes). heat the remaining oil in another frying pan and sauté the spring onions for 1 minute, add the cabbage and bean sprouts and continue to cook for a couple of minutes.

Add the bean curd, noodles and peanut sauce. Mix thoroughly and cook over a low heat for a couple of minutes.

makes 4 portions

ravishing risotto

To make a traditional risotto is very time-consuming as the liquid is added to the rice about four times during the cooking period. Anyone with children to look after will know that cooking something which involves a lot of attention and precise timing can quickly result in a very burnt saucepan. With this recipe the liquid is added all at once and the rice can happily be left to simmer in a covered saucepan for 30 minutes. You can add all kinds of vegetables to this basic risotto – just lightly sauté leeks, mushrooms, red peppers, courgettes or your child's favourite vegetables and add with the Parmesan towards the end of the cooking time, as described below.

1 large onion, peeled and finely chopped
40 g (1¹/₂ oz) butter or margarine
225 g (8 oz) easy cook brown rice
1.2 litres (2 pints) chicken or vegetable stock (see pages 33–4)

175 g (6 oz) frozen peas
50 g (2 oz) freshly grated Parmesan cheese
¹/₄ teaspoon freshly grated nutmeg
Freshly ground black pepper

Sauté the onion in the butter or margarine over a medium heat in a heavy-bottomed casserole until soft (about 5 minutes). Rinse the rice thoroughly under cold running water, add to the onion and stir with a wooden spoon until well coated with butter. Pour over the chicken stock or vegetable stock, bring to the boil, then cover and simmer for 15 minutes. Remove the lid, simmer for 10 minutes more, then add the peas and continue to cook for a further 5 minutes (check from time to time and add extra stock if necessary). At the end of the cooking time there may still be some liquid left in the rice. Add the Parmesan, nutmeg and a little pepper and stir very well for a couple of minutes. If left to stand, the excess liquid will soon be absorbed by the warm rice.

makes 5 portions

PERFECT PASTA

Most children adore pasta. It's fun to eat and easy to chew. Fresh-cooked pasta in a myriad of different shapes, colours and sizes, served with a delicious home-made sauce made from fresh natural ingredients makes a quick, easy and cheap meal for the whole family. Pasta combines well with almost any food and children can be enticed to eat lots of different nutritious foods which they might never touch were they not served with pasta.

There is a wonderful variety of pasta to choose from. You can buy fresh ravioli stuffed with ricotta and spinach and serve it with a home-made tomato sauce. You can stuff cannelloni with minced chicken, vegetables or meat. In my local supermarket I can buy pasta in the shape of space ships, animals or cars and you can even teach your child to read by serving alphabet pasta.

Individual pieces of pasta like pappardelle (bow-tie shaped) or penne (tubular) are easier for young children to eat than long strands of spaghetti. However, my three-year-old daughter has invented her own method of coping with spaghetti – she holds it out in front of her by the two ends, bites in the middle and sucks both ends into her mouth. Not the height of good manners perhaps, but certainly very effective!

pasta with chicken and peppers au gratin

Chicken with pasta is quite unusual but this creamy pasta with a golden,
bubbly topping makes a great combination.

1 chicken breast, cut into small strips
Salt and freshly ground black pepper
Vegetable oil or margarine for frying
½ small red pepper, de-seeded and cut
into strips
½ small yellow pepper, de-seeded and
cut into strips

25 g (1 oz) butter or margarine
25 g (1 oz) flour
250 ml (8 fl oz) milk
50 g (2 oz) Parmesan cheese, grated
50 g (2 oz) thin dried spaghetti or fresh
pasta

Season the chicken with a little salt and pepper and sauté for about 2 minutes
in the oil or margarine. Add the peppers and sauté together with the
chicken for 3 to 4 minutes until the chicken is cooked through.

To prepare the sauce, melt the butter or margarine and stir in the flour over
a low heat, stirring constantly for 2 to 3 minutes. Take the pan off the heat and
vigorously stir in the milk. When the sauce is well blended, stir over a medium
heat until it is thick and smooth. Off the heat, stir in 35 g (1¼ oz) of the
Parmesan cheese and season lightly with salt and pepper (remember the cheese
will already make the sauce quite salty).

Cook the pasta in a large pan of boiling water but leave it a little undercooked
as it will be cooked again when it is placed under the grill. Drain well and mix
with the chicken, peppers and cheese sauce and put it into an ovenproof dish.
Sprinkle the remaining cheese over the top of the pasta and place under a hot
grill for a few minutes until the topping is brown and bubbly.

makes 2 portions

tasty tomato sauce for pasta

Pasta with tomato sauce is always popular with children and this recipe for tomato sauce can be used as the basis for many different pasta dishes. It's worth making this sauce in a large quantity and then freezing in small portions. For a tasty variation, sauté a chopped pepper with the onion and add a small aubergine (sliced into rounds) and lightly fried. Then chop the sauce for a few seconds in a food processor. Combined with a béchamel sauce and some Parmesan cheese it also makes a lovely, creamy sauce.

1 small onion, peeled and finely chopped
1 clove garlic, finely chopped (optional)
1 tablespoon finely chopped fresh parsley
1 tablespoon olive oil
3 tomatoes, skinned, de-seeded and chopped (optional)

1 × 800-g (1 lb 12-oz) tin tomatoes, drained and chopped
2 tablespoons tomato purée
1 tablespoon fresh basil leaves
¼ teaspoon dried oregano
Salt and freshly ground black pepper

Sauté the onion, garlic (if using) and parsley in the olive oil until soft but not browned (about 5 minutes). Add the rest of the ingredients and cook over a low heat for about 15 minutes.

makes about 350 ml (12 fl oz) sauce

tagliatelle with haddock, cheese and tomato

This is a great recipe for encouraging your child to eat more fish. You could use other white fish like hake or cod instead of haddock.

275 g (10 oz) haddock
Salt and freshly ground black pepper
Knob of butter or margarine
1 tablespoon lemon juice
1 small onion, peeled and finely sliced
1 tablespoon chopped fresh parsley
65 g (2½ oz) cooked frozen or fresh peas (optional)
3 medium tomatoes, peeled and sliced

2 tablespoons tomato purée
20 g (¾ oz) butter or margarine
1½ tablespoons flour
250 ml (8 fl oz) milk
¼ teaspoon freshly grated nutmeg
65 g (2½ oz) grated mature Cheddar cheese
100 g (4 oz) spinach tagliatelle
15 g (½ oz) grated Parmesan cheese

To cook the fish, place it in a microwave dish, season lightly, dot with butter or margarine and pour over the lemon juice. Lay the onion slices on top and sprinkle over the parsley. Microwave on high for 5 minutes turning the fish halfway through. Alternatively, bake the fish and onion in an ovenproof dish at gas mark 4, 350°F (180°C) for 10–15 minutes. Check to make sure the fish is cooked through, then flake with a fork, removing any bones. Mix the flaked fish, onions, parsley, peas (if using) and cooking liquid with the sliced tomatoes and tomato purée.

While the fish is cooking prepare the cheese sauce. Melt the butter or margarine in a saucepan and stir in the flour to make a roux. Let it cook for 1 minute. Gradually stir in the milk to make a thick white sauce and season with nutmeg. Off the heat, stir in the cheese.

Pre-heat the oven to gas mark 4, 350°F (180°C), if necessary. Cook the pasta in a large pan of boiling water (but leave it a little on the hard side as it will be cooked again in the oven). Drain well and mix with the cheese sauce. In a greased ovenproof dish, put a layer of pasta followed by a layer of fish in tomato sauce. Repeat until all the ingredients have been used. Sprinkle the top with Parmesan. Cook for 10 minutes and then brown under a hot grill for a couple of minutes.

makes 4 portions

FABULOUS FISH

Fish is a wonderful food for children, it's high in protein, low in fat, has a nice soft texture for lazy chewers and it's quick to cook. It's a shame that many children are confirmed fish-haters. My theory is that often children aren't given the chance to develop a liking for fish and have maybe been put off by being given bland or overcooked fish. Once a child decides he doesn't like a particular food, it's jolly hard to persuade him otherwise.

I have tried to put together a collection of tasty fish recipes to encourage children to be excited at the prospect of fish for dinner. Many of the recipes combine fish with favourite foods like Fish-shaped salmon cakes with tasty tomato sauce (see page 87), and fruity fish (see page 86) combining fish fillets with bananas and grapes, and many more. There are several fish recipes in other sections of this book including ideas for combining pasta with fish and even a recipe for fish finger pie!

Don't forget to flake fish carefully before giving it to your child to make sure there are no bones.

mermaid morsels

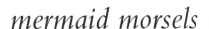

I tell my children that these miniature fish balls are Ariel's favourite food –
Ariel being the mermaid in the Disney *Little Mermaid* film. I think this
recipe is one of the tastiest ways of giving your child fish. If you freeze
these once they are cooked you can simply remove as many as you need
and leave to defrost for a delicious meal. Best served cold. You can use any
combination of whatever white fish is available – cod, haddock, whiting,
hake or halibut. A fishmonger should be able to prepare it for you. A
variation to try: leave out the coating of flour and simmer the balls in the
Tasty tomato sauce for pasta on page 82 for a really scrumptious meal.

2 onions, peeled and finely chopped
Vegetable oil and butter or margarine for
frying
1 kg (2 lb) minced or finely chopped
white fish
1 large carrot, scrubbed and finely
chopped
1 Granny Smith apple, peeled and
grated

1 tablespoon finely chopped fresh
parsley (optional)
2 eggs
2 tablespoons sugar
2 teaspoons salt
¼ teaspoon freshly ground black pepper
85 ml (3 fl oz) cold water
2 tablespoons flour plus extra for rolling

Fry the onions in a mixture of oil and butter or margarine until soft and
golden (about 6–7 minutes). Combine minced fish, fried onions, carrot,
grated apple and parsley (if using). Beat the eggs together with the sugar, salt
and pepper using an electric whisk until frothy and add the egg mixture to the
minced fish. Finally, mix in the cold water and flour.

Form into small balls, roll in flour and fry in a mixture of vegetable oil and
butter or margarine until golden.

makes about 40 balls

flaked fish with bananas and grapes

Blending fruit with fish gives it a taste which children love. This is quick
and easy to make and lovely served over a bed of rice.

225 g (8 oz) haddock, hake, cod or
plaice, cut into chunks
Salt and freshly ground black pepper
Butter or margarine for frying
2 bananas

10 seedless grapes, peeled
15 g (½ oz) butter or margarine
1 tablespoon flour
150 ml (5 fl oz) milk

Season the fish with a little salt and pepper. Sauté the fish in butter or margarine until it flakes easily with a fork. Meanwhile, peel the bananas and cut them in half lengthwise and in half again. Fry them in butter until soft and golden. Combine the fish, bananas and grapes. Make a white sauce in the usual way, season with a little salt and pepper and pour this over the fish. Simmer for 4 to 5 minutes. Serve over a bed of rice.

makes 3 portions

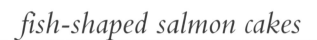

fish-shaped salmon cakes

This is a simple way to turn fish cakes into a special treat. They are good surrounded by a red sea of Tasty tomato sauce for pasta (see page 82).

350 g (12 oz) potato
225 g (8 oz) salmon fillets or 200 g
(7 oz) tinned salmon or tuna
Salt and freshly ground black pepper
Squeeze of lemon juice
A few sprigs of parsley
A knob of butter
2 tablespoons tomato ketchup

A few drops of Worcestershire sauce
(optional)
1 heaped teaspoon snipped fresh chives or
finely chopped parsley or spring onion
1 egg, beaten
Crushed cornflakes for coating the fish
cakes
Sunflower oil

Peel the potato, cut it into pieces and boil until soft. Set aside until cool. To cook the salmon, pre-heat the oven to gas mark 4, 350°F (180°C), place the fillets in foil, season lightly with salt and pepper, add lemon juice and parsley and dot with the butter. Wrap loosely and bake for 15 to 20 minutes. Alternatively, cook the salmon in a microwave in a dish covered with cling film. (Cook, covered, on high for 3½ to 4½ minutes.)

Remove the skin from the salmon, drain away any juices and mash with a fork taking care to make sure that there are no bones. Alternatively, flake the tinned fish. Add the potato and mash this together with the fish, tomato ketchup, Worcestershire sauce (if using), chives or spring onion.

With floured hands, form the mixture into 6 oval fish cakes, then pinch in one end to form the tail of a fish. Brush with beaten egg and coat in the crushed cornflakes. Lightly fry or place on a greased baking sheet, brush with oil and bake for 20–25 minutes, turning after about 10 minutes.

makes 6 fish cakes

salmon kedgeree

I use fresh salmon for this recipe but you could substitute tinned salmon or smoked haddock. I use an ice-cream scoop to make 'castles' of kedgeree for my children and they love it.

150 g (5 oz) rice
175 g (6 oz) fresh salmon
40 g (1½ oz) butter or margarine
Squeeze of lemon juice
½ small onion, peeled and chopped
1 tablespoon flour
250 ml (8 fl oz) milk

½ bay leaf
¼ teaspoon grated nutmeg
1 teaspoon mild curry powder
Salt and freshly ground black pepper
1 or 2 hard-boiled eggs, chopped
2 tomatoes, skinned, de-seeded and chopped

Cook the rice in boiling, lightly salted water until tender. Drain and set aside. Meanwhile, put the fish in a dish, dot with 15 g (½ oz) of the butter or margarine and squeeze over some lemon juice. Cover with cling film and microwave on medium high for 4 to 5 minutes, turning halfway through. Alternatively wrap the fish loosely in silver foil and bake for about 15 minutes in the oven at gas mark 4, 350°F (180°C).

To prepare the sauce, melt the remaining butter or margarine and sauté the onion until soft. Stir in the flour to make a roux and cook for 1 minute. Gradually add the milk, stirring until the sauce thickens. Add the bay leaf, nutmeg, curry powder and salt and pepper and simmer for a couple of minutes. Flake the salmon taking care to remove any bones and add the fish to the sauce, having first removed the bay leaf. Stir in the chopped hard-boiled egg(s), chopped tomato and cooked rice.

makes 5 portions

pass the parcel

Bringing these parcels of scrumptious fish to the table will certainly arouse your child's curiosity. Serve with mashed potatoes or rice. You could use haddock, cod, hake or sole instead of plaice if you prefer.
For another simple but very delicious parcel, take a fillet of fish, sprinkle over 1 tablespoon of chopped spring onions, 1 tablespoon of soy sauce and dot with butter or margarine. Wrap in foil and cook as below.

225 g (8 oz) fillets of plaice
Salt and freshly ground pepper
4 medium tomatoes, skinned, de-seeded
and chopped or 1 × 400-g (14-oz) tin
tomatoes, drained

50 g (2 oz) Cheddar cheese, grated
25 g (1 oz) cornflakes, crushed
2 tablespoons milk
A knob of butter or margarine

Pre-heat the oven to gas mark 4, 350°F (180°C).
Place the fillets on foil and lightly season. Mix together the tomatoes, cheese, cornflakes and milk and cover each of the fillets with some of the sauce.

Dot with margarine and wrap up into separate parcels (use greaseproof paper instead if cooking in the microwave) and cook in the oven for about 15 minutes or for about 4 minutes on high in a microwave. The fish will flake easily with a fork when cooked. Make sure there are no stray bones, mash the fish together with the sauce, and serve.

makes 4 portions

tuna with sea-shells

Tuna is cheap and nutritious – it's worth keeping a tin in the larder for emergencies and this tasty recipe is popular and quick to make. Finish off with cheese on top or leave plain. If your child is not too keen on tuna, then resort to disguise and chop the sauce into small pieces in a food processor.

175 g (6 oz) multi-coloured pasta shells
1 onion, peeled and finely chopped
1 clove garlic, peeled and crushed
Olive oil for frying
½ red and ½ green pepper, de-seeded and chopped

1 × 400-g (14-oz) tin tomatoes, drained and chopped
2 tablespoons tomato purée
½ teaspoon dried oregano
1 small tin tuna, drained and flaked
2 tablespoons double cream or milk
40 g (1½ oz) Cheddar cheese, grated

Cook the pasta in boiling water until cooked but firm. Sauté the onion and garlic in the olive oil until soft, then add the peppers and sauté for 2–3 minutes. Add the chopped tomatoes, tomato purée and oregano, bring to the boil and simmer for about 4 minutes. Add the tuna, heat through and then mix in the cream. Place the pasta in an ovenproof dish, pour over the sauce and sprinkle the Cheddar cheese on top, brown under a pre-heated grill taking care not to burn.

makes 3–4 portions

Chomping Chicken

Chicken is the staple diet of my family. It is cheaper to buy than other meat or fish, low in fat and so versatile that you could eat chicken almost every day of the week and still not be bored with it. Chicken or turkey offers the same high quality protein as meat. It is also a good source of vitamin B which promotes growth, energy, healthy skin and keeps the nervous system in balance. The dark meat of chicken supplies the most iron. The subtle flavour of moist tender chicken can be combined with other foods to appeal to almost every taste.

Diced chicken can be stir-fried in 5 minutes and a boneless breast of chicken takes no more than about 8 minutes to cook. However, chicken should never be served undercooked, make sure that the meat is opaque and white. If the chicken is properly cooked, then it should be tender and bursting with juices.

Plain roast chicken served with a good gravy and roast potatoes is always a family favourite in my house and I've given a few recipes for using up left-over cold chicken. Children love to chew on chicken drumsticks, but watch young children to make sure that they do not choke on small pieces of bone. You can combine chicken with fruit, rice, vegetables or pasta and why not tempt your child with one of the more unusual recipes like Nasi goreng (on page 96), an Indonesian recipe combining chicken with rice and peanuts.

tasty chicken stir-fry

Both my older children love stir-fried chicken. There are many different vegetable combinations that you can use but as a short-cut you can buy a packet of pre-prepared stir-fry vegetables in most supermarkets and add a few of your child's favourite vegetables too.

2 boned chicken breasts
4 tablespoons vegetable oil
1 medium onion, cut into thin slices
1 medium carrot, cut into strips
175 g (6 oz) cauliflower, cut into small florets
175 g (6 oz) baby corn, cut in half lengthways
1 small green pepper and 1 small red pepper, de-seeded and cut into strips
175 g (6 oz) courgettes, cut into strips
175 g (6 oz) beansprouts
175 g (6 oz) shredded Chinese cabbage
½ chicken stock cube, finely crushed
2 tablespoons oyster sauce
Salt and freshly ground black pepper

100 g (4 oz) fine Chinese noodles (optional)
250 ml (8 fl oz) chicken stock or water (optional with the noodles)
2 tablespoons sesame seeds toasted in a dry frying pan

MARINADE
2 tablespoons soy sauce
1 teaspoon sugar
1 tablespoon sesame or vegetable oil
2 tablespoons sake or dry sherry (optional)
2 spring onions, finely sliced
Freshly ground black pepper

Cut the chicken into bite-sized pieces. Combine the ingredients for the marinade and marinate the chicken for at least 30 minutes. Heat 2 tablespoons of the oil in a wok or frying pan and sauté the chicken for about 5 minutes. Remove the chicken with a slotted spoon and set aside. Heat the remaining oil in the wok. Add the onion and sauté for 3–4 minutes then add the carrot, cauliflower and baby corn and cook for 3 minutes. Add the green and red pepper, courgettes, beansprouts and Chinese cabbage and cook for a further 3 minutes. Return the cooked chicken to the pan, add half a crumbled stock cube, pour over the oyster sauce and season to taste.

If you wish to add noodles, bring 250 ml (8 fl oz) of stock or water to the boil, stir in the noodles, cover the pan and allow to simmer for 3 minutes, gently stirring with a fork. Drain and mix the noodles with the chicken and vegetables.

Finish off by sprinkling with toasted sesame seeds.

makes 6 portions

chicken drumsticks with barbecue sauce

Chicken drumsticks are fun for your child to hold and eat. Simply wrap the ends in foil and they can be eaten either hot or cold.

½ small onion, finely chopped
Margarine or oil for frying
1 teaspoon lemon juice
2 teaspoons malt vinegar
1 teaspoon brown sugar

2 tablespoons tomato purée
A few drops of Worcestershire sauce
Salt and freshly ground black pepper
2 chicken drumsticks

Sauté the onion in the margarine or oil until soft, then stir in the lemon juice, vinegar, sugar, tomato purée and Worcestershire sauce. Simmer gently for 3 to 4 minutes and season lightly. Remove the skin from the drumsticks, make 2 deep cuts in each and brush all over with the sauce. Place on a piece of foil and cook under a pre-heated medium grill for about 20 minutes, turning frequently and basting with the sauce.

makes 2 portions

chicken and potato pancake

A delicious thick golden crispy pancake with a soft succulent centre. This recipe can be varied by adding other vegetables like grated courgettes or chopped sweet peppers. I make it in a 20-cm (8-inch) frying pan and my children enjoy cutting their own slices – it can be eaten either hot or cold.

*1 chicken breast, cut into pieces or some
left-over cooked chicken
300 ml (10 fl oz) chicken or vegetable
stock (see pages 33–4)
1 baking potato, peeled and grated
1 onion, peeled and grated*

*40 g (1½ oz) frozen peas
1 small egg, beaten
1 tablespoon flour
Salt and freshly ground black pepper
2 tablespoons vegetable oil*

Poach the chicken breast in the stock until cooked through (15–20 minutes). Press out the liquid from the grated potato and combine the potato with the onion, frozen peas, egg and flour and season lightly with some salt and pepper. Dice the chicken and add it to the vegetable mixture.

Heat 1 tablespoon of oil in the frying pan, tilt the pan so that the oil coats the sides, and press the mixture into the pan. Fry for about 5 minutes or until browned. Turn the pancake onto a plate. Heat the rest of the oil, and brown the pancake on the other side for about 7 minutes. Cut into wedges and serve.

makes 4 portions

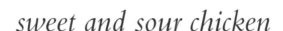

sweet and sour chicken

Sweet and sour chicken is a great favourite with young children and this sauce is also very good with fish. Serve on a bed of rice.

Salt and freshly ground black pepper
3 chicken breasts, cut in half
Vegetable oil for frying
1 large onion, peeled and finely chopped
1 green pepper, de-seeded and cut into fine strips
1 red pepper, de-seeded and cut into fine strips

1½ tablespoons cider vinegar or red wine vinegar
2 tablespoons tomato purée
1 small tin pineapple chunks in syrup
8 ml (3 fl oz) water
2 tablespoons soy sauce
½ teaspoon ground ginger (optional)
1 tablespoon cornflour

Pre-heat the oven to gas mark 4, 350°F (180°C).

Season the chicken breasts lightly and fry in the oil until lightly browned. Drain on kitchen paper.

Sauté the onion in a little oil for 3 to 4 minutes, then add the peppers and continue to cook for a further 2 minutes and set aside.

Combine the vinegar, tomato purée, 50 ml (2 fl oz) pineapple syrup from the can of pineapples, water, soy sauce and ginger (if using) and stir until well mixed. Put the chicken breasts into a casserole dish, cover with this mixture, and stir in the onion and peppers. Bake the chicken for 20 minutes. Add the pineapple chunks and bake for a further 10 minutes. Remove the chicken and pour the sauce into a saucepan. Mix the cornflour with a little cold water and stir this into the sauce, bring to the boil and simmer until the sauce is thickened.

Remove the chicken from the bone, cut it into small pieces, cover with the sauce and serve.

makes 6 portions

nasi goreng N

This is a delicious Indonesian recipe flavoured with peanuts and a mild curry sauce. It is a great favourite with the whole family.

2 chicken breasts, skinned and off the bone, cut into chunks
2 tablespoons soy sauce
50 ml (2 fl oz) sesame or vegetable oil
1 large onion, peeled and finely chopped
2 teaspoons curry powder
1/2 teaspoon turmeric
350 g (12 oz) basmati rice
900 ml (1 1/2 pints) chicken or vegetable stock (see page 33–4)

Vegetable oil for frying
3 spring onions, finely chopped
1 red pepper, de-seeded and finely chopped
90 g (3 1/2 oz) baby sweetcorn, cut in half lengthways
100 g (4 oz) frozen peas
1 tablespoon molasses
1/2 cup roasted peanuts, finely chopped

Marinate the chicken in the soy sauce for at least 1 hour. In a large saucepan, heat the oil, add the onion, curry powder and turmeric and sauté for 5 minutes. Add the rice and continue to stir and cook for a further 5 minutes until it has turned golden. Add the stock and simmer, covered, for 20 to 25 minutes or until the rice is tender.

Meanwhile in a wok or saucepan, fry the chicken in the vegetable oil for about 3 minutes. Add the spring onions, red pepper and baby sweetcorn and pour over the soy sauce from the chicken marinade. Cook the vegetables for about 2 minutes then add the frozen peas. Continue cooking for a further 3 to 4 minutes. Combine the chicken and vegetables with the rice and stir in the molasses and chopped peanuts. Simmer for about 5 minutes.

makes 8 portions

Florentine chicken strips

This dish freezes well, so I usually make 3 or 4 individual portions from this recipe. As a variation you could add 100 g (4 oz) sliced button mushrooms sautéed in a little butter to the sauce.

3 chicken breasts, cut into strips
Salt and freshly ground black pepper
50 g (2 oz) butter or margarine
450 g (1 lb) fresh or 225 g (8 oz)
frozen spinach
1½ tablespoons flour

300 ml (10 fl oz) chicken or vegetable
stock (see pages 33–4)
120 ml (4 fl oz) single cream or milk
50 g (2 oz) Cheddar cheese, grated
¼ teaspoon grated nutmeg
25 g (1 oz) Parmesan cheese, grated

Pre-heat the oven to gas mark 4, 350°F (180°C).
Season the chicken with a little salt and pepper and sauté in 25 g (1 oz) of the butter or margarine for 3 to 4 minutes. Meanwhile cook the spinach and squeeze out the excess water. Put the spinach into one or several greased ovenproof dishes and place the strips of chicken on top.

To make the sauce, melt the remaining butter or margarine, add the flour and cook for 1 minute. Gradually add the chicken or vegetable stock, stirring constantly to make a thick sauce. Bring to the boil then remove from the heat. Stir in the cream or milk, Cheddar cheese, grated nutmeg and season with a little salt and pepper. Pour this sauce over the chicken and sprinkle with Parmesan. Cook in the oven for 10 minutes.

makes 3–4 portions

cold chicken with sweet curry sauce ❄

This is my favourite recipe for using up left-over chicken. It's great served with rice and my children like it when I cut the chicken into cubes and thread the pieces onto skewers.

½ onion, peeled and chopped
1 tablespoon corn oil
1 dessertspoon curry powder
2 tablespoons apricot jam
1 teaspoon lemon juice
50 ml (2 fl oz) chicken or vegetable
stock (see pages 33–4)

½ teaspoon tomato purée
1 bay leaf
120 ml (4 fl oz) mayonnaise
`1 heaped tablespoon raisins
275 g (10 oz) cooked chicken pieces,
cut into chunks

Sauté the onion in the oil until soft and add the curry powder. Simmer for 1 minute, then stir in the apricot jam and lemon juice and cook gently for 1 minute more. Pour over the stock, add the tomato purée and the bay leaf and simmer for 2 minutes. Remove from the heat, take out the bay leaf and beat in the mayonnaise. Stir in the raisins, pour the sauce over the chicken and serve.

makes 4 portions

grandma's chopped liver

There is a tendency for parents who dislike liver not to make it for their children but you should not show your dislike of certain foods as your child will be inclined to mimic you. It is better for your child to experiment for himself and make his own choices.

This is a tasty way of making liver for your child, I spread it onto fingers or mini triangles of toast and sprinkle over the chopped egg. It can also be used for sandwich fillings. I make it in bulk and then freeze it in small portions and it comes in handy as a nutritious meal or snack.

1 medium onion, peeled and finely chopped
2 tablespoons vegetable oil

225 g (8 oz) chicken livers
2 hard-boiled eggs chopped
Salt and freshly ground black pepper

Sauté the onion in the oil until golden. Meanwhile grill the chicken livers until cooked through (about 5 minutes). Mix together with 1½ of the chopped eggs, keeping the remainder for decoration, and season to taste with a little salt and pepper.

makes 8 portions

super satay chicken N

Satay is a natural for peanut-butter lovers and it's a great sauce for beef, prawns or chicken. Of course, eating food off a stick is always very appealing to children, so this recipe is a real winner.

2 large chicken breasts
120 ml (4 fl oz) chicken stock
120 g (4¹/₂ oz) crunchy peanut butter
1 teaspoon soy sauce
1 tablespoon sake or sherry

1 tablespoon honey
1 teaspoon curry powder
¹/₂ teaspoon turmeric
2 tablespoons onion, finely chopped
1 small clove garlic, crushed

Cut the chicken breasts into chunks. Mix all the rest of the ingredients together to make the sauce and bring it to the boil and simmer for 5 minutes. Marinate the chicken in the sauce for several hours or refrigerate and leave overnight. Thread three or four pieces of chicken on to each skewer and grill or barbecue them for 20 minutes or until cooked, turning frequently and basting occasionally with the sauce.

makes 6 skewers

Nicholas's chicken on a stick N ✳

My son Nicholas loves this recipe. The chicken pieces are deliciously moist and it's very appealing if you thread them onto bamboo skewers with chunks of steamed vegetables like baby corn and red pepper in between.

For the mild curry dip
1/2 *small onion, peeled and chopped*
vegetable oil
1/2 *tablespoon mild curry powder*
1 *teaspoon soft brown sugar*
1 *tablespoon flour*
120 *ml (4 fl oz) chicken stock (see page 33)*

For the peanut dip
3 *tablespoons peanut butter*
120 *ml (4 fl oz) coconut milk*
1/2 *tablespoon soy sauce*
1 *tablespoon lemon juice*
a little ground cayenne pepper
(optional)

2 *chicken breasts*
1 *egg white*
1 *tablespoon light soy sauce*
1 *tablespoon cornflour*
seseame oil or sunflower oil

Combine all the ingredients in a saucepan and cook stirring for 3–4 minutes. This dip will keep for a few days in the fridge.

To make the mild curry dip, sauté the onion in the oil until soft. Stir in the curry powder and sugar. Add the flour and continue stirring, gradually adding the chicken stock until thickened.

Cut the chicken diagonally into strips, or into chunks if you are going to thread it onto a skewer. Whisk together the egg white, soy sauce, sake and cornflour, add the chicken and mix weel. Heat the oil in a wok or frying pan and sauté the chicken until cooked through.

To make the peanut dip, combine all the ingredients in a saucepan and cook stirring for 3–4 minutes. This dip will keep for a few days in the fridge.

makes 2 portions

MEATY MENUS

More and more people are turning away from red meat in favour of fish or chicken. If you choose to do this, bear in mind that red meat provides vitamin B12 and more iron and zinc than either fish or poultry. Red meat provides the best source of iron and iron deficiency is the commonest nutritional deficiency in the developing world. Good quality red meat should be quite safe to give to young children but you should avoid processed meats and sausages.

I find that children tend to prefer recipes made with minced meat rather than chunks of meat which are difficult to chew. Make sure that when you buy minced meat, there is very little fat. You can always ask your butcher to mince some lean cuts of beef especially for you. A good tip is to chop the minced meat in a food processor once it has been cooked to make it even softer for your child to chew. If you are making a stew or goulash, trim the meat first to cut away the fat and any tough pieces of sinew, and cook in a slow oven for several hours so that it is tender.

If your child is reluctant to eat meat, then try making a tasty meat and tomato sauce and serve this over pasta. I have found that many children who would not normally touch meat are quite happy to eat it when it is combined with something that they enjoy like pasta or rice.

Children also love to eat from their own individual portions. If you are making a Shepherd's pie for the whole family, reserve a little to make a separate dish for your child. This is much more appetizing than a portion just dolloped onto a plate.

succulent leek and meat croquettes

These mini-burgers are soft and juicy. They have a delicious flavour and are very simple to make.

2 leeks, white part only, carefully washed
25 g (1 oz) butter
225 g (8 oz) lean minced beef
1 Granny Smith apple, peeled and grated

1 teaspoon Marmite
Salt and freshly ground black pepper
Vegetable oil for frying

Thinly slice the leeks and sauté in the butter until lightly golden and softened. Put the minced beef and cooked leeks into a food processor and chop for a few seconds on pulse. Put the meat mixture into a bowl and mix in the grated apple, Marmite and seasoning. Using your hands, form into about 12 croquettes and sauté in vegetable oil until cooked.

makes about 12 croquettes

lamb chops baked in a parcel ✳

This is a very easy recipe which seals in all the flavour of the chops. Some children are quite happy chewing meat, especially if they can chew it off a bone. You could also serve the chops with the barbecue sauce on page 93.

¼ small onion, peeled and finely chopped
1 small potato, peeled and cut into small cubes
½ small green pepper, de-seeded and chopped
Vegetable oil for frying

2 lamb rib chops
½ teaspoon Marmite
1 medium tomato, peeled and finely chopped
Salt and freshly ground black pepper
A knob of butter or margarine

Pre-heat the oven to gas mark 4, 350°F (180°C).
Sauté the onion, potato and green pepper lightly in vegetable oil. Meanwhile place the chops on a piece of silver foil. Smear each one with Marmite, then cover with the sautéed vegetables and chopped tomato. Season lightly with salt and pepper and dot with butter or margarine. Fold the foil around the chops and bake for 1 hour.

makes 2 portions

miniature meatballs

Children love the taste of these tiny meatballs. I stick cocktail sticks into them and my children love biting them off the sticks. However, make sure you are watching them so that they do not end up poking the sticks into each other! This recipe is good served with rice and meatballs are an excellent standby in your freezer. You can dress them up and serve them mixed with spaghetti in the Tasty tomato sauce for pasta on page 82 or serve them with the sweet and sour sauce from the recipe on page 95.

500 g (18 oz) lean minced beef
2 tablespoons chopped fresh parsley
2 slices brown bread, made into breadcrumbs, 50 g (2 oz)
1 onion peeled and finely chopped
1 garlic clove, crushed (optional)

2 Granny Smith apples, peeled and grated
1 crumbled chicken stock cube, dissolved in 50 ml (2 fl oz) water
Freshly ground black pepper and salt to taste

Pre-heat the oven to gas mark 4, 350°F (180°C).
Mix all the ingredients together well, seasoning lightly. Shape into small balls. Place the balls on 2 oiled baking trays and cook in the oven for 20 minutes. Alternatively you can lightly fry the meatballs in vegetable oil until they are browned and then simmer them for 15 minutes in one of the sauces mentioned above.

makes about 40 meatballs

triple decker shepherd's pie

This recipe makes 6 mini-portions of shepherd's pie, which I freeze and use for a quick ready-made meal. Children love brightly coloured peas and sweetcorn and I have used them here as the tempting filling between meat and potato (you could also use baked beans). Instead of the cheeses you could use 25 g (1 oz) butter or margarine in the mashed potato.

750 g (1¹/₂ lb) lean minced beef
1 small garlic clove, crushed (optional)
Vegetable oil
1 large onion, peeled and chopped
1 green pepper, de-seeded and chopped
1 red pepper, de-seeded and chopped
225 g (8 oz) mushrooms, washed and sliced
1 x 800-g (1 lb 12-oz) tin tomatoes, chopped
1 beef or chicken stock cube

175 ml (6 fl oz) water
Marmite
A few drops Worcestershire sauce (optional)
6 medium-sized potatoes, peeled and cut into chunks
50 ml (2 fl oz) milk
275 g (10 oz) mixed peas and sweetcorn
50 g (2 oz) margarine

Brown the minced beef and garlic (if using) in vegetable oil then chop it for a few seconds in a food processor to make it soft to chew. Meanwhile, sauté the onion until soft, then add the green and red peppers and mushrooms and sauté for 3 to 4 minutes. Combine the beef with the onions and peppers and add the chopped tomatoes with their juices. Dissolve the stock cube in the water and add it, together with the Marmite and some Worcestershire sauce, if using. Simmer gently for about 20 minutes.

Meanwhile, boil the potatoes for about 20 minutes or until soft, and cook the peas and sweetcorn. Mash the potatoes with the milk and 40 g (1¹/₂ oz) of the butter. Pre-heat the oven to gas mark 4, 350°F (180°C).

Spread the meat in 6 individual ramekins, cover with a layer of peas and sweetcorn and top with mashed potato. Cook in the oven for about 20 minutes. Then dot the top with the remaining butter and put under a hot grill for about 3 minutes until brown and crispy.

<u>*makes 6 portions*</u>

Scarlett's tasty rice meal

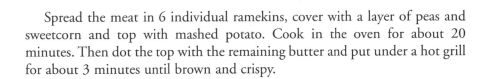

A complete meal for your child that is simple, healthy and very tasty. My two-year-old daughter loves this dish even though she is not keen on eating red meat.

75 g (3 oz) basmati rice
1 onion, peeled and chopped
Vegetable oil for frying
225 g (8 oz) lean minced beef
1/2 red or green pepper, de-seeded and chopped
1 tablespoon chopped fresh parsley
1 tablespoon tomato purée

Salt and freshly ground black pepper
2 tomatoes, skinned, de-seeded and chopped
75 g (3 oz) frozen peas
175 ml (6 fl oz) chicken or vegetable stock (see pages 33–4)
120 ml (4 fl oz) pure apple juice

Cook the rice in boiling water until tender. Drain well. Sauté the onion in the oil for 2 to 3 minutes. Add the minced meat and cook, stirring, until browned. Add the pepper, parsley, tomato purée and light seasoning and cook for another 3 to 4 minutes. Add the tomatoes and frozen peas, pour over the stock and apple juice, cover and simmer for about 15 minutes. Stir in the cooked rice 5 minutes before the end of the cooking time.

<u>*makes 3 portions*</u>

Hungarian goulash

The secret of a good Hungarian goulash is to leave it to cook for a long time at a low heat to ensure that the meat is really tender. It is delicious served with noodles or rice.

Salt and freshly ground black pepper
Flour for coating
450 g (1 lb) lean braising steak, cut into small cubes
Vegetable oil for frying
3 small or 2 large onions, peeled and finely sliced
1 red pepper, de-seeded and cut into strips

1 green pepper, de-seeded and cut into strips
1 tablespoon paprika
1 × 800-g (1 lb 12-oz) tin tomatoes, drained and chopped
2 tablespoons tomato purée
2 tablespoons chopped fresh parsley
300 ml (10 fl oz) chicken, beef or vegetable stock (see pages 33–4)
3 tablespoons soured cream or yoghurt

P re-heat the oven to gas mark 2, 300°F (150°C).
   Season the flour lightly and roll the beef cubes in it. Fry them in the oil until browned on all sides. Meanwhile, sauté the onions until soft, add the peppers and cook these for 2 to 3 minutes. Sprinkle over the paprika and continue to cook for about 2 minutes.

Put the meat and vegetables into a casserole and add all the remaining ingredients except the soured cream or yoghurt. Cover and cook in the oven for at least 3 hours, stirring occasionally. Finally stir in the soured cream or yoghurt before serving.

makes 6 portions

FRUITY FANTASIES

There is nothing more delicious or better for your child than fresh ripe fruit. It makes great finger food and none of the vitamins and nutrients are destroyed through cooking. My son Nicholas adores fruit so much that we have to hide the fruit bowl until he finishes his main course. Try and encourage your children to eat fruit rather than sickly sweet puddings and chocolates.

Present fresh fruit in an appealing way to your child. Make it look attractive, choose contrasting colours of fruit, cut the fruit into interesting shapes and arrange the fruit in patterns on the plate (see illustrations). Always make sure that you remove any stones before giving fruit to your child – he could so easily choke and it is important to keep fruit like lychees out of the reach of curious young children.

Where raw fruit is concerned, there are endless variations on a theme. Purée or grate fruits and mix them with cottage cheese, yoghurt or fromage frais. Cut the fruit into bite-sized chunks, thread on a skewer to make fruit kebabs and maybe serve with a dipping sauce like yoghurt and honey or fromage frais mixed with fruit purée. Make jellies (you can make your own with fruit juice and gelatine) and add fresh fruit – berries are good set in blackcurrant juice. Make a banana sandwich – simply cut a banana in half lengthways, spread one side with cream cheese and press a layer of granola on top. Cover with the other half of the banana and cut in two. Dried fruits left to soak in boiling water make good finger food or serve a dried fruit compote with hot custard (see the chapter Scrumptious snacks for more ideas).

Try giving your children some more exotic fruits like persimmon which looks like an orange tomato and tastes a little like a plum. It works well mixed with cottage cheese or fromage frais and can be found in large supermarkets when it is in season. Papaya and mango also blend well with dairy produce. Kiwi fruit is a good source

of vitamin C and makes a good snack peeled and cut into slices. Let your child try the slightly tart taste of some fruit desserts like apples and blackberries or gooseberries and you may be surprised how much he enjoys them.

On a hot day there is nothing nicer than some Home-made ice lollies (see page 115). They are much better for your child than some of the highly coloured, artificially flavoured commercial lollies on sale.

winter fruit salad

A mixture of various dried fruits – apple rings, dried apricots, prunes and maybe peaches and pears – can be bought in packets in most supermarkets. Add some fresh fruits and maybe some dates, raisins or even toasted pine nuts or use your child's favourite dried fruits.

225 g (8 oz) mixed dried fruits
175 ml (6 fl oz) unsweetened apple or grape juice
175 ml (6 fl oz) water
1 apple, cored, peeled and cut into slices

2 oranges, peeled and cut into segments with the pith removed
4 plums, peeled, stoned and cut into slices or 1 large pear, peeled and cut into slices
1 banana, peeled and cut into slices

Simmer the dried fruits in the fruit juice and water for about 10 minutes. Then add the prepared fresh fruit and simmer for a further 3–4 minutes.

makes 5 portions

apple snowman ❄

This is a great way to turn a baked apple into a special treat for children.

2 cooking apples, cored
2 tablespoons raisins
1 tablespoon soft brown sugar
½ teaspoon cinnamon
15 g (½ oz) butter or margarine
2 teaspoons apricot jam

6 tablespoons water
1 egg white
1 teaspoon castor sugar
2 blueberries, 2 raisins, 1 strawberry,
1 kiwi fruit for decoration

Pre-heat the oven to gas mark 4, 350°F (180°C).

Score all the way around the skin of the apple, this will stop the apple skin bursting in the oven. Stuff the apples with the raisins. Sprinkle with the brown sugar and cinnamon and dot with butter or margarine. Place 1 teaspoon of jam on top of each apple. Put the apples onto an ovenproof dish and pour the water around the base of the apples. Bake for 45 minutes.

After 15 minutes, whisk the egg white until it stands up in soft peaks. Add the castor sugar and beat again until stiff (taking care not to over-beat). Divide the egg white in two and put a dollop on each of the apples. Baste the apples with the liquid in the bottom of the dish and continue to bake for the remaining 30 minutes. Decorate using the fruit with the kiwi fruit as the hat.

makes 2 portions

baked pears ❄

A simple but tasty recipe. Instead of fresh pears you could use
a tin of pear halves.

4 ripe pears, peeled, cored and halved
Brown sugar
Butter or margarine for dotting

200-g (7-oz) carton Greek yoghurt or
double cream

Pre-heat the oven to gas mark 4, 350°F (180°C).
Place the pears hollow side up in a baking dish. Put a little brown sugar inside each pear and top with a knob of butter or margarine (you will need more sugar if using yoghurt). Pour over the yoghurt or cream and bake for about 10 minutes.

makes 4 portions

cinnamon apple pie

This makes a delicious dessert served hot with ice-cream.

50 g (2 oz) margarine
120 g (4½ oz) soft brown sugar
1 egg, beaten
100 g (4 oz) self-raising flour
Pinch of salt
50 ml (2 fl oz) milk

2 large cooking apples, peeled and cut
into slices
2 tablespoons raisins
½ teaspoon cinnamon
¼ teaspoon mixed spice
1 tablespoon water

Pre-heat the oven to gas mark 4, 350°F (180°C).

Cream together the margarine and 50 g (2 oz) of the sugar and gradually fold in the beaten egg. Sift together the flour and salt and gradually fold this in together with the milk, to make a soft sticky batter.

Mix the apple slices with the remaining sugar, raisins, cinnamon and mixed spice and cover the base of a 20-cm (8-inch) pie dish. Add the water. Spoon the batter over the apples and spread it around as evenly as possible. If there are gaps, you will find that the batter will spread anyway once it is in the oven. Cook for about 40 minutes.

makes 8 portions

triple berry fool ❋

This is a delicious recipe for berries which aren't quite sweet enough to eat on their own – I serve it in tall glasses and it looks spectacular.

225 g (8 oz) blackberries, fresh or frozen
225 g (8 oz) raspberries, fresh or frozen
225 g (8 oz) strawberries, fresh or frozen

40 g (1½ oz) castor sugar
120 ml (4 fl oz) double cream
175 ml (6 fl oz) Greek yoghurt

Put half the fruit into a saucepan with the sugar and 1 tablespoon of water and simmer for 3 to 4 minutes. Put the cooked berries through a mouli to get rid of all the seeds. Beat the cream until thick, stir in the fruit purée when cool (it will turn a wonderful purple colour), and swirl in the yoghurt to make a patterned fool. Spoon some of the remaining fresh berry mixture into each glass and mix with enough sugar to sweeten. Top with the fruit fool.

makes 4 portions

baked blackened bananas ❋

This is one of my favourite desserts and it's terribly simple to make.
Children are fascinated to see the skin of the banana turn black! They are
fabulous served hot with vanilla ice-cream.

3 large or 4 small bananas
25 g (1 oz) unsalted butter or
margarine
25 g (1 oz) brown sugar

85 ml (3 fl oz) freshly squeezed orange
juice
1 tablespoon lemon juice
¼ teaspoon ground cinnamon

Pre-heat the oven to gas mark 6, 400°F (200°C).
Cut a slit lengthwise in the skin of each banana, and place on a baking
sheet. Bake in the oven for about 15 minutes or until the skins turn black.
Meanwhile, melt the butter or margarine over a gentle heat and stir in the rest
of the ingredients. Bring to the boil and cook bubbling for about three
minutes. Peel the cooked bananas and add these to the sauce for 3 to 4 minutes,
basting well and turning.

makes 2 portions

home-made ice lollies

In summer when your toddler is hot and bothered and off his food, the one thing that will tempt him to eat is a nice cool ice-cream and I find that often what they won't eat on a plate they will eat frozen at the end of a stick. Plastic ice lolly moulds are cheap to buy and available in most supermarkets. Simply pour the chosen mixture into the mould (cover with the top, which is also the stick) and once frozen run under the hot tap to remove. These are far removed from the commercial lollies full of artificial colouring, flavourings and E numbers.

FROZEN BERRY POP
Simmer mixed berries, e.g. raspberries, blueberries and blackberries with a little icing sugar. Pass the mixture through a sieve and mix with some blackcurrant juice.

RAINBOW POP
Freeze in three stages. You need one layer each of orange juice, blackcurrant juice and pineapple or passion fruit juice.

MANGO MUNCHKIN
Blend together 1 small carton of Greek yoghurt, 1/2 ripe mago and honey to taste.

RASPBERRY RIPPLE
Make a raspberry purée by blending together some fresh raspberries and icing sugar to sweeten. Sieve the purée and swirl into whole milk vanilla or peach yoghurt.

FRESH FRUIT SALAD LOLLY
Blend together 120 ml (4 fl oz) freshly squeezed orange juice, 1 pear, 1 peach and 1 small banana.

TROPICANA
Blend together 1 orange (cut in segments, pith removed),1 peach, 1 mango and the juice of 4 passion fruits.

WATERMELON CRUSH
Remocve the seeds from some chunks of sweet watermelon and blend with some strawberry yoghurt.

VERY STRAWBERRY LOLLY
Purée 150 g (5 oz) strawberries with a little icing sugar. Press through a sieve to de-seed. Mix with two (40 g/1 1/2 oz) mini-pots of strawberry fromage frais.

Lovely Lunch-boxes

Less than half the children in this country have school dinners so it's important that lunch-boxes provide a tasty and nutritious alternative. In 1998, the caterer Gardner Merchant found in their survey on children's eating habits that crisps or similar savoury packet snacks were the most common item in a packed lunch box and whereas 39 per cent of children took a chocolate bar to school in their lunch-box, very few children brought fresh fruit. A high fat, high salt, refined carbohydrate meal such as this diminshes mental alertness, may lead to obesity and your child will probably end up tired towards the end of the day. Also a diet high in saturated fat and salt can lay the foundations for heart disease and high blood pressure later in life.

Children don't care how healthy their food is. If it doesn't appeal to them, they won't eat it. Biscuit cutters in the shape of toys or animals can make sandwiches or other foods into delightful treats. Your child will be much more enthusiastic about a teddy bear-shaped sandwich, which will arouse a lot of interest from his classmates! Put the food into colourful paper bags, thread cheese, fruit or vegetables onto skewers (food is much more fun if it can be eaten off a stick), or even draw a face on the skin of a banana with a felt pen. Touches like these will mean a lot to your child and will encourage him to eat.

With a little imagination, you can make delicious lunch-boxes with lots of variety. Organization is the key and a lot of things can be prepared the day before or even frozen. Last night's dinner is always a good starting point – mini chicken balls, chicken and pasta salad or a tasty tomato soup in a thermos flask. To keep a sandwich or salad fresh in hot weather, buy a mini-ice pack to put in the lunch-box, which you can pop in the freezer overnight and it will stay frozen for eight hours.

Let your child help choose what goes into his lunch-box and, if you have time, involve him in the preparation. There are lots of ideas for sandwich fillings on pages 140–180. I hope the following list will give you other ideas for your child's lunch-box:

- *miniature cheeses*
- *tuna and pasta salad with mayonnaise and sweetcorn*
- *super satay chicken on a skewer* 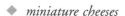 *(page 100). Yakitori chicken and satay chicken can also be bought in supermarkets*
- *raisins and cashew nuts (only give whole nuts to older children)* **N**
- *twin cartons of cream cheese with miniature breadsticks*
- *yoghurt and mini-yoghurt drinks*
- *fromage frais in mini-pots or tubes*
- *fruity kebabs made with different fruits*
- *raw vegetable sticks with a dip (use an empty pot of yoghurt and cover with foil for the dip)*
- *slice of pizza*
- *rolled-up slices of turkey or chicken, secured with a cocktail stick*
- *hard-boiled eggs, sliced in half, then the yolk mashed with cream cheese, chopped liver or creamy salmon, tuna or chicken and wrapped in cling film*
- *slices of cheese cut into shapes with biscuit cutters*
- *stuffed pockets: small round pitta breads stuffed with different fillings are very popular with children. Try egg mayonnaise or tinned tuna or salmon mixed with mayonnaise and some chopped spring onions or a slice of meat loaf*

The following recipes elsewhere in this book also make good lunch-box food:

- *Mock baked beans (page 49)*
- *Blissful banana bread* **N** *(page 66)*
- *Tasty tomato soup (page 71)*
- *Onion soup with floating stars (page 72)*
- *Delicious vegetable rissoles (page 74)*
- *Cheese, onion and tomato tart (page 76)*
- *Mermaid morsels (page 85)*
- *Tasty chicken stir-fry (page 92)*
- *Chicken drumsticks with barbecue sauce (page 93)*
- *Chicken and potato pancake (page 94)*
- *Chicken with sweet curry sauce (page 98)*
- *Miniature meatballs (page 105)*
- *Cheddar cheese muffins (page 128)*
- *Best-ever oatmeal raisin cookies (page 134)*
- *Golden apple and raisin muffins* **N** *(page 135)*
- *Carrot and pineapple muffins* **N** *(page 136)*
- *Tasty rice meal (page 170)*

chicken and pasta salad with sweetcorn

This is the most delicious, easy-to-prepare chicken salad. It's great for a child's lunch-box or for a light lunch in summer.

600 ml (1 pint) chicken stock
2 chicken breasts
100 g (4 oz) pasta twirls, cooked and cooled
100 g (4 oz) tinned or frozen sweetcorn
18 small cherry tomatoes, cut in half
2 spring onions, finely sliced
1/2 baby gem lettuce, shredded

Dressing
3 tablespoons olive oil
1 tablespoon white wine vinegar
1/2 teaspoon Dijon mustard
1/2 teaspoon sugar
Salt and freshly ground black pepper
1 tablespoon chicken stock from the poaching liquid

Poach the the chicken for about 10 minutes in the stock, then leave to cool completely. Remove the chicken with a slotted spoon and cut into bite-sized pieces (this can be prepared the night before). To make the dressing, whisk together all of the ingredients (or use a hand blender). Combine all the ingredients for the salad and toss in the dressing.

makes 5 portions

sweet chicken salad parcel ❄

50 g (2 oz) cooked chicken, chopped
1 tablespoon grated Gruyère or
Emmenthal cheese
1 teaspoon finely sliced spring onion
(optional)

1 tablespoon drained crushed pineapple
or chopped tinned peaches
A little shredded lettuce
1 tablespoon mayonnaise
1 small round pitta bread

Simply mix all the ingredients and stuff inside the pitta bread.

makes 2 portions

chicken balls with apples and courgettes

Combining chicken with apples brings out a flavour that children love.

2 chicken breasts, cut into pieces
½ small onion, peeled and grated
1 small courgette, topped and tailed,
washed and grated
2 Granny Smith apples, peeled and
grated

Squeeze of lemon juice
4 tablespoons wheatgerm
1 chicken stock cube, crumbled
½ beaten egg
Salt and freshly ground black pepper
Vegetable oil for frying

Combine all the ingredients together except the last three and chop in a food processor. Add the beaten egg, season and mix well. Form into walnut-sized balls and fry in vegetable oil until golden brown. Alternatively the balls can be poached in chicken stock or tomato sauce for about 8 minutes.

makes about 15 balls

vermicelli omelette

Children love pasta and this is a good way of making it part of their lunch-box. The recipe below uses onion, red pepper and peas, but you could make up your own combination using your child's favourite vegetables and maybe some grated cheese. Eat the rest yourself or simply freeze cut portions so that they are on hand when you need them.

1 small onion, peeled and chopped
½ red pepper, de-seeded and chopped
Butter or margarine for frying
75 g (3 oz) vermicelli

3 eggs, beaten
25 g (1 oz) Parmesan cheese, grated
Salt and freshly ground black pepper
65 g (2½ oz) frozen peas

Sauté the onion and pepper in butter or margarine until soft. Meanwhile cook the vermicelli in boiling water. When it is ready, drain and chop it. Season the beaten eggs lightly with salt and pepper and add the onion, pepper, peas, vermicelli and cheese. Melt about 15 g (½ oz) butter or margarine in a 20-cm (8-inch) heavy-bottomed frying pan and tilt the pan so that the sides are coated half-way up. Then fry the egg mixture over a gentle heat for about 8–10 minutes (or until the omelette is lightly browned underneath). To finish, brown under a hot grill for about 3 minutes.

makes 6 portions

pasta salad with apple dressing ✳

The secret of this recipe is to choose a fun-shaped pasta – I've found animal pasta and spaceship pasta in my local supermarket! If you don't have a steamer, you can use steaming baskets in ordinary saucepans – just start the sweetcorn and red pepper cooking 3 minutes later than the broccoli and cauliflower.

150 g (5 oz) fun-shaped pasta
1 chicken breast
150 ml (5 fl oz) chicken or vegetable stock (see pages 33–4)
50 g (2 oz) cauliflower
50 g (2 oz) broccoli
1 courgette
50 g (2 oz) frozen sweetcorn

¼ red pepper, de-seeded and finely chopped
1½ tablespoons balsamic or wine vinegar
2 tablespoons apple juice
2 tablespoons olive oil
Salt and freshly ground black pepper
1 heaped tablespoon chopped spring onion or chives

Cook the pasta until tender in boiling water. Cut the chicken breast into small pieces and poach in the stock until cooked through (about 8 minutes). Meanwhile, prepare the vegetables and steam in a two-tiered steamer. Broccoli and cauliflower below, courgette, sweetcorn and red pepper on top. Steam for about 6 minutes – vegetables should still be crisp.

To prepare the dressing, whisk the vinegar together with the apple juice, oil and light seasoning, then add the spring onion or chives. Combine the cooked, drained pasta with the vegetables and chicken and toss in the dressing.

makes 4 portions

chicken soup with rice and vegetables

I find that children like soups that are full of lots of different ingredients and this recipe is a good way to get your child to eat a really healthy meal. I like to add some mild curry powder to this soup – it is surprising how many children like the flavour of curry.

2 chicken breasts on the bone
2.25 litres (4 pints) chicken or vegetable stock (see pages 33–4)
1 medium onion, peeled and finely chopped
1 stalk of celery, finely chopped
1 carrot, peeled and finely chopped
Vegetable oil for frying

100 g (4 oz) basmati rice
1 small green pepper, de-seeded and finely chopped
2 tomatoes, peeled and finely chopped
1 tablespoon mild curry powder
1 tablespoon tomato purée
Salt and freshly ground black pepper

Cook the chicken breasts in the stock for about 20 minutes or until tender. Sauté the onion, celery and carrot in vegetable oil for about 3 minutes, add the rice and green pepper and continue to cook for 3 minutes. Add the tomatoes, curry powder and tomato purée and simmer for a couple of minutes. Add the vegetables to the chicken stock, lightly season the soup and simmer for 30 minutes. Remove the skin and bones from the chicken and chop up the meat. Add the chopped chicken to the soup and simmer for 3 to 4 minutes before serving.

makes about 8 portions

SCRUMPTIOUS SNACKS

If your child eats three good meals a day then you are a very lucky mother indeed. For the rest of us we need to supplement our child's diet with healthy snacks. Often children just do not have the patience to sit down and eat a proper meal. Little children's stomachs are small and it is difficult for them to eat enough at breakfast to last them to lunchtime when they have been rushing around all morning. Snacks are therefore a very important part of a child's diet.

If you encourage your child when he is very young to enjoy eating healthy snacks like fresh fruit, carrot sticks or slices of cheese instead of bars of chocolate, sweets or ice-cream, it is likely that he will continue these habits later in life and enjoy a much healthier diet.

Don't forget that many savoury shop-bought snacks are not much better than sweet ones. They consist mainly of puffed-up, artificially flavoured and coloured cereals, high in fat and salt and which have next to no nutritional value. Many of the additives used are not permitted by law in foods for babies and young children, although the products are made to appeal to young consumers. If you do buy crisps, look out for the increasing range of lower-fat and lightly salted varieties. Even so, these still often contain high levels of salt and fat.

Good snack recipes elsewhere in the book are Carrot and pineapple muffins (page 136), Golden apple and raisin muffins (page 135), Sesame tofu fingers (page 76), Mermaid morsels (page 85), Grandma's chopped liver (page 99), Chicken sausages (page 118), Chicken balls with apples and courgettes (page 119) and Stuffed pockets (page 117)

fruit snacks

When it is available try some more exotic fruits like mango, lychees, papaya, sharon and kiwi fruits (a good source of vitamin C). Mixed berries or redcurrants are also good fruits to try and, if they are not very sweet, add a tiny sprinkling of icing sugar.

A fun way of giving fruit to your child is to pile an assortment of chopped fruits into an ice-cream cone and on a hot day put a scoop of vanilla ice-cream underneath.

For a special treat a very appealing way of giving fruit to children is to melt some dark chocolate and some white chocolate in separate pans. Dip the tip of the fruit into the chocolate and pierce the fruit with a cocktail stick. Stick the cocktail sticks with the fruit into an orange and put this into the fridge to allow the chocolate to harden on the fruit. Strawberries, pineapple chunks and orange or tangerine segments are especially nice but you must eat them the same day. If you are worried about your child having too much chocolate, use carob as a substitute. (Carob has no caffeine in it and it is lower in calories, fat content and salt.) Remember to remove the cocktail sticks before giving the fruit to your children.

You can also combine fruit with other healthy foods – for example, cottage cheese with chopped pineapple or a cracker with peanut butter and apple **N**.

caged monsters

These are fun snacks which look wonderful and only take 5 minutes to make. Older children will enjoy making up their own monsters with your help, using whatever ingredients you happen to have (see illustration).

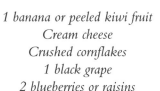

1 banana or peeled kiwi fruit
Cream cheese
Crushed cornflakes
1 black grape
2 blueberries or raisins

1 date or grape
1 large orange
1 dessertspoon salad cress, chopped
Cocktail sticks

Peel the banana and cut a 6 cm (2½ inch) chunk from the top of the banana or follow the recipe using a whole ripe kiwi fruit. Spread some cream cheese over the banana with a knife and roll it in the crushed cornflakes. Cut 2 slices of grape for the eyes, stick these on the banana with a blob of cream cheese and in the centre of these, stick on the blueberries or raisins again using the cream cheese. Stick in a date or grape for a nose.

Cut 2 thick slices from the centre of a large orange. Put the monster on top of one of these slices and surround with the salad cress. Put cocktail sticks around the edge of this slice to make the 'bars' of the cage and then place the other slice so that it is balanced on top of the sticks to form a roof.

Once my children have let the monster out of his cage, I cut the orange slices in half and they can eat these too.

makes 1 caged monster

three blind mice on toast

This fun snack looks like three blind mice hiding under a blanket. I got the idea for this from an American cookbook. It's a great way of getting your child to eat cheese and tomatoes on toast and terribly easy to make.

1 piece of brown bread
Butter or margarine for spreading
6 cherry tomatoes

2 slices of cheese (e.g. Gruyère)
6 curly pretzels or some cooked strands
of spaghetti

Toast the bread and spread with butter or margarine, cut the toast in half. Cut a thin slice off the bottom of the tomatoes so that they stand up. Arrange 3 in a row on the edge of each piece of toast. Put the 2 cheese slices on top of the tomatoes (see illustration).

Place the toast on a non-metal plate in the microwave and cook on high for about 30 seconds or until the cheese has melted. Alternatively, cook under a pre-heated grill for about 1 minute or until the cheese melts. Stick a pretzel or a strand of cooked spaghetti under the cheese for the tail.

makes 2 × three blind mice!

vegetable spaghetti

This never fails to impress! You can add a few chopped herbs if you like.

1 large carrot, peeled
1 large courgette, trimmed

Butter or margarine for frying

Pare both the carrot and the courgette into long thin ribbons using a potato peeler. Melt a little butter or margarine in a frying pan and sauté the vegetable spaghetti for about 3 minutes.

serves 2

fruity kebabs

Children love food on sticks and for special occasions you can dip the fruit into chocolate. If you are making several kebabs stick them into a large orange or grapefruit. Supervise young children as kebab sticks can be sharp. Make the kebabs from a selection of the following ingredients. Apples and bananas will need to be sprinkled with lemon juice to prevent them turning brown.

chunks of cheese, chunks of cooked chicken, cherry tomatoes, chunks of cucumber, chunks of apples, grapes,

strawberries, pineapple chunks, melon chunks, chunks of peeled kiwi fruit, chunks of banana, dried fruits

fluffy cheese and tomato toast ✳

This is simple and quick to prepare and so delicious that I can't resist making an extra one for Mum too! For variation, you can substitute 50 g (2 oz) sliced sautéd mushrooms for the tomato.

1 tomato, skinned, seeded and chopped
15 g (½ oz) butter or margarine
1 egg

40 g (1½ oz) Cheddar cheese, grated
2 pieces of wholemeal bread, toasted

Sauté the tomato in the butter for about a minute. Separate the egg and mix together the yolk, the grated cheese and the cooked tomato. Beat the egg white until stiff and fold this into the cheese mixture. Pile onto two slices of toast and place under a pre-heated grill until fluffy and golden.

makes 2 portions

Cheddar cheese muffins

For variation, add one large grated carrot or some cooked sweetcorn. These freeze well and you can simply take out as many as you need, cover with foil and re-heat in the oven.

2 eggs
50 ml (2 fl oz) vegetable oil
120 ml (4 fl oz) natural fromage frais
2 tablespoons maple syrup
75 g (3 oz) matured Cheddar cheese, grated

1 teaspoon mustard powder
120 g (4½ oz) plain flour
65 g (2½ oz) wholewheat flour
1½ teaspoons baking powder
½ teaspoon bicarbonate of soda
½ teaspoon salt

Pre-heat the oven to gas mark 4, 350°F (180°C).
Combine the first five ingredients. In a separate bowl, sift together the dry ingredients. Fold these into the cheese mixture, taking care not to voermix. Spoon into a muffin tray lined with paper cases. Bake for about 20 minutes.

makes 12 muffins

Mr banana face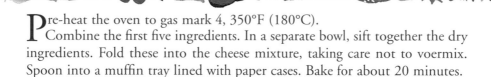

Rice cakes are popular with children, I think it is the texture they like. Combining a rice cake with this nutritious topping makes an amusing snack.

1 rice cake
Peanut butter, cream cheese or
fromage frais

Slices of banana
1 cherry tomato
Raisins

Spread the rice cake with some peanut butter or cream cheese or fromage frais, arranges slices of banana for the eyes, a cherry tomato for the nose and raisins for a smile.

makes 1 portion

animal dips

Tasty dips with raw vegetables, sesame sticks, crackers, crisps or parboiled vegetables make a wonderful snack for children of all ages. It's simple to decorate the dips to make them look like animal faces – the colour of the dip will give you inspiration: avocado for a frog, peanut for a lion, cream cheese and tomato for a pig (see the illustration). A few minutes spent on presentation will make all the difference!

Try your child with some of the following for dipping: scrubbed carrot sticks, strips of red, yellow or green pepper, raw cauliflower florets, cucumber sticks, slices of avocado, sticks of celery, cherry tomatoes, radicchio (red lettuce) or chicory.

peanut lion dip N ❄

This works with fruit as well as vegetables.

3 tablespoons Greek yoghurt
3 tablespoons cream cheese
3 tablespoons peanut butter
1 tablespoon maple syrup
Matchstick crisps, sesame sticks, cooked spaghetti, strips of yellow pepper or celery

Carrot sticks
1 slice of mushroom
2 olives or 2 pieces of shaped cheese
2 blueberries
Red pepper or tomato

Simply mix the yoghurt, cream cheese, peanut butter and syrup together and then decorate: make a mane using the matchstick crisps or one or a combination of the alternatives; whiskers with the carrot sticks; a nose with the mushroom slice, and form eyes with the olives or cheese (using the blueberries for the centre). Finally place a strip of red pepper or tomato to make a mouth.

<u>*makes 250 ml (8 fl oz)*</u>

avocado frog dip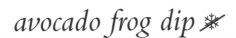

You can use 2 slices of cucumber with slices of egg and olive on top for the eyes and stripes of chives for the mouth.

1 ripe avocado
2 tablespoons finely chopped onion
1 tablespoon finely chopped red pepper
Squeeze of lemon juice

1 tablespoon snipped chives
2 tablespoons cream cheese
Salt and freshly ground black pepper

Cut the avocado in half, remove the stone and scoop out the flesh. Mash or blend all the ingredients together, seasoning lightly.

makes 250 ml (8 fl oz)

lucky dip

A good idea when you are out and about with the children is to make up little snack bags, using brightly coloured miniature carrier bags and filling them with lots of different healthy foods. Below are some of the foods you might choose – it makes a healthy alternative to a bag of crisps.

Miniature wrapped cheeses
Cherry tomatoes
Dried fruits like apple rings, dates,
apricots, raisins, banana chips
Carrot, celery or cucumber sticks

Grapes, plums, apple slices
Healthy breakfast cereals
Sesame sticks
Whole-grain foods like unsweetened
popcorn, wheat or rye crackers

BISCUITS, CAKES AND MUFFINS

So many mothers reach for the biscuit tin to find their child a between meal snack. Supermarket shelves are full of a tempting array of brightly coloured iced biscuits, chocolate-coated teddy bears and jam tarts. These attractively packaged biscuits designed specifically to appeal to children are likely to contain nothing but empty calories and do nothing but harm to your child's diet, spoiling his appetite for more wholesome foods and promoting tooth decay.

Why not make your own delicious home-baked cakes and biscuits? At least you will know *exactly* what your child is eating. With a little imagination and some fun-shaped biscuit cutters there is no reason why they should not be every bit as appealing to your child as the shop-bought variety and there are many recipes in this section which are quick and easy to make. Muffins are very popular with my children – they're packed full of good wholesome ingredients and children like the fact that they get their own individual one to eat.

chewy chocolate oatmeal cookies N

Simple to make but hard to resist! You can also make these cookies using white chocolate buttons, raisins or chopped dried fruit in place of the chocolate chips.

100 g (4 oz) butter or margarine
75 g (3 oz) brown sugar
75 g (3 oz) granulated sugar
1 egg
1 tablespoon milk
1 teaspoon vanilla essence
100 g (4 oz) plain wholemeal flour

1/2 teaspoon baking powder
1/2 teaspoon bicarbonate of soda
1/2 teaspoon salt
75 g (3 oz) rolled oats
65 g (2 1/2 oz) pecans, roughly chopped
150 g (5 oz) plain chocolate chips

Cream the butter or margarine with the sugars. Beat in the egg, milk and vanilla. Sift together the flour, baking powder, bicarbonate of soda and salt and beat this into the mixture. Finally stir in the oats, chopped pecans and chocolate chips. Cover and refrigerate the dough for at least 1 hour.

Pre-heat the oven to gas mark 4, 350°F (180°C). Line 4 baking sheets with non-stick baking parchment. Form the dough into walnut-sized balls and flatten slightly onto the baking sheets, making sure they are spaced well apart. Bake for 12 to 15 minutes. They will still be quite soft but will harden once they have cooled down.

makes about 24 cookies

best-ever oatmeal raisin cookies

These and Chewy chocolate oatmeal cookies (see page 133) are my favourite home-made biscuits. Mummy and Daddy gobble them up before the children get a look in!

75 g (3 oz) butter or margarine
40 g (1½ oz) brown sugar
25 g (1 oz) granulated sugar
½ beaten egg
1 tablespoon water
1 teaspoon vanilla essence
40 g (1½ oz) plain wholemeal flour

½ teaspoon cinnamon or mixed spice
Pinch of salt
¼ teaspoon bicarbonate of soda
75 g (3 oz) oat flakes or quick-cooking rolled oats
75 g (3 oz) raisins

Pre-heat the oven to gas mark 4, 350°F (180°C).

Cream the butter or margarine with the sugars. Beat in the egg and add the water and vanilla. Sift together the flour, mixed spice, salt and bicarbonate of soda. Mix this into the egg mixture. Finally stir in the oats and raisins.

Line 3 baking sheets with non-stick baking parchment. Make walnut-sized balls of dough and flatten these down onto the baking sheet – you may want to enlist the 'help' of your child for this stage. Bake for about 15 minutes, until the edges are done but the centres are still soft.

makes about 15 cookies

golden apple and raisin muffins N

These delicious muffins are full of goodness and deliciously tempting.
Serve them for tea or as a snack for your child at any time
during the day.

100 g (4 oz) plain or wholemeal flour
1 teaspoon baking powder
2 teaspoons bicarbonate of soda
50 g (2 oz) soft brown sugar
1/4 teaspoon salt
1 teaspoon ground cinnamon
75 g (3 oz) bran flakes, crushed

1 egg
120 ml (4 fl oz) milk
120 ml (4 fl oz) apple juice
85 ml (3 fl oz) vegetable oil
100 g (4 oz) raisins
50 g (2 oz) chopped pecans or walnuts
1 apple, peeled and grated

Pre-heat the oven to gas mark 4, 350°F (180°C).
In a large bowl, sift together the flour, baking powder, bicarbonate of soda, brown sugar, salt and cinnamon. Add the crushed bran flakes. In another bowl, beat together the egg, milk, apple juice and vegetable oil. Gradually stir the liquid ingredients into the flour mixture, taking care not to over-mix and finally fold in the raisins, nuts and (if using) apple.

Line 2 muffin trays with paper cases. Fill each case about 2/3 full with the batter and bake for approximately 16 to 20 minutes. The muffins are ready when a cocktail stick inserted in the centre comes out clean.

makes about 10 muffins

carrot and pineapple muffins

These muffins are irresistible – they're my family's favourite snack and are always popular when children come over for tea. They can be served plain or iced with cream cheese icing for special occasions.

100 g (4 oz) plain flour
100 g (4 oz) plain wholemeal flour
1 teaspoon baking powder
3/4 teaspoon bicarbonate of soda
1 1/2 teaspoons ground cinnamon
1/2 teaspoon salt
250 ml (8 fl oz) vegetable oil
90 g (3 1/2 oz) caster sugar
2 eggs
120 g (4 1/2 oz) grated carrots (about 2 carrots)

1 x 225-g (8-oz) tin crushed pineapple, drained
100 g (4 oz) raisins

For the cream cheese icing
50 g (2 oz) softened unsalted butter
50 g (2 oz) icing sugar
1/2 teaspoon vanilla essence
100 g (4 oz) cream cheese

Pre-heat the oven to gas mark 4, 350°F (180°C). Sift together the flours, baking powder, bicarbonate of soda, cinnamon and salt and mix well. Beat the oil, sugar and eggs until well blended. Add the grated carrots, crushed pineapple and raisins. Gradually add the flour mixture, beating just enough to combine all the ingredients.

Pour the batter into muffin trays lined with paper cases and bake for 25 minutes. Cool.

To prepare the icing, cream together the butter, icing sugar and vanilla essence. Stir in the cream cheese by hand and spread the mixture evenly over the muffins.

makes about 12–14 muffins

heavenly chocolate mousse cake

This is a good recipe to prepare with your child for a special occasion.

175 g (6 oz) digestive biscuits
40 g (1¹/₂ oz) butter or margarine
150 ml (5 fl oz) boiling water
65 g (2¹/₂ oz) lemon jelly
100 g (4 oz) good quality plain chocolate

225 g (8 oz) cream cheese
50 g (2 oz) caster sugar
2 eggs, separated
Cocoa powder for decoration

Crush the biscuits in a food processor, Melt the butter or margarine and stir into the crushed biscuits. Line an 18- or 20-cm (7- or 8-inch) cake tin with baking parchment and press the crumbs down evenly over the base.

Pour the boiling water over the jelly and stir until dissolved. Set aside to cool then put in the fridge until it just begins to set. Melt the chocoale and then beat the cream cheese with the sugar, egg yolks and melted chocolate. Whisk the egg whites until stiff. Fold the semi-set jelly into the chocolate mixture together with the egg whites. Pour over the biscuit base and put the cake in the fridge to set. Sift cocoa powder over just before serving.

chocolate peanut butter crisp **N** ❄

This makes a scrumptious treat for lovers of peanut butter. If you prefer, you can leave out the chocolate.

5 tablespoons smooth peanut butter
50 ml (2 fl oz) maple syrup
1 teaspoon vanilla extract

90 g (3¹/₂ oz) rice crispies
100 g (4 oz) milk chocolate

Gently heat the peanut butter and maple syrup and stir in the vanilla extract. Add the rice crispies, mixing well with a spatula until well coated. Grease a 20-cm (8-inch) square cake tin and press the rice crispie mixture firmly into the tin with the back of a wooden spoon. Melt the chocolate in a microwave or double boiler, set aside to cool and then spread over the top of the rice crispie mixture. Once cool, put in the fridge to set and serve cut into small squares.

makes 12 squares

apple and date munch and crunch N

This is a cross between a pudding and a cake, so you could serve it for tea or after a meal – one thing's for sure, there won't be much left over! It's especially good with fresh dates which can sometimes be bought in the supermarket.

40 g (1 oz) butter
50 g (2 oz) brown sugar
1 egg
100 g (4 oz) wholemeal self-raising flour
A pinch of salt

1 large cooking apple, peeled, cored and diced
100 g (4 oz) stoned dates, chopped (about 6 dates)
50 g (2 oz) pecans or walnuts, chopped

Pre-heat the oven to gas mark 4, 350°F (180°C). Beat the butter with the sugar and add the egg. Add the flour and the salt. Fold in the fruit and nuts and spread the mixture into a greased shallow tin 20 cm (8 inch) square. Bake in the oven for about 30 minutes.

makes 6 portions

banana upside-down cake N

A lovely moist cake with a delicious topping – cut it into squares and serve as a pudding or tea-time treat.

90 g (3¹/₂ oz) butter or margarine
120 g (4¹/₂ oz) brown sugar
5 bananas, peeled and sliced
75 g (3 oz) raisins
75 g (3 oz) whole pecans, cut into quarters

2 eggs, beaten
1 teaspoon vanilla essence
225 g (8 oz) self-raising flour
2 teaspoons baking powder
¹/₂ teaspoon salt
85 ml (3 fl oz) milk

Pre-heat the oven to gas mark 4, 350°F (180°C).
Melt 40 g (1¹/₂ oz) of the butter or margarine in a saucepan and stir in 40 g (1¹/₂ oz) of the brown sugar until melted. Spread this mixture over the base of a shallow 20-cm (8-inch) square non-stick cake tin. Arrange the sliced bananas, raisins and pecans on top.

Cream together the remaining butter or margarine and sugar. Beat in the eggs and vanilla. Sift together the dry ingredients and gradually beat these into the first mixture alternately with the milk until smooth. Pour the batter over the bananas, don't worry if there are some gaps as the batter will spread when cooked.

Bake for 40 to 45 minutes. Turn out upside-down whilst still warm.

<u>*makes 12 portions*</u>

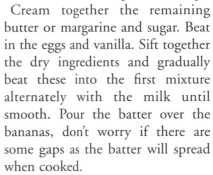

TEA PARTIES AND SPECIAL TREATS

Amazing isn't it that when we celebrate a happy event, such as a birthday or tea party, we serve up particularly unhealthy food — sausages, fancy crisps and cakes with coloured icing. Parents are trying against considerable odds to prevent their children from getting a taste for food that undermines their health. Why do 'bad' foods always have to be treats, why not 'good' foods for a change?

It is much more satisfying seeing children tucking-in with relish to a selection of home-made goodies. Your child will enjoy eating the food all the more if you allow him to 'help' you make it in the kitchen. Just remember it will probably take you twice as long!

Organization is obviously very important and it's possible to make and freeze most of the biscuits and cakes so that you can limit your work on the day. All that you should then need to do is make the sandwiches, ice the cake, lay the table and get Dad to blow up the balloons.

With a little imagination, sandwiches can be just as appealing to your child as cookies and cream cakes. Sandwiches need not only be served for tea, but can make a quick, easy meal for your child. There are so many different breads available in supermarkets now — olive bread, foccacia, rye bread — they almost fill the whole aisle. There are all sorts of homemade fillings you can try. It is surprising what a child will eat inside a fancy-shaped sandwich that he would never touch if it were served to him on a plate!

Presentation is important, you can have a lot of fun designing novelty sandwiches and there are lots of ideas for fun-shaped party food like jelly boats and animal dips (see pages 146 and 129) which are simple to make. You can cut a watermelon into the shape of an animal and fill it with fruit (see illustration) which makes a healthy alternative to a bowl of Smarties. Scale everything down because children love miniature food and they like to try lots of different things! Make mini muffins and cookies (see pages 133 to 136)

It's a lot of fun designing sandwiches in all shapes and sizes. Biscuit cutters are a very simple way of transforming a simple sandwich into something special for your child. Small animal-shaped biscuit cutters are always popular and you can give the animals eyes, whiskers and tails, where appropriate, using raisins, carrots, cucumber or whatever else comes to hand. Larger biscuit cutters like those used to make gingerbread men are great for open sandwiches.

Even those parents with the most limited artistic flair can try their hand at novelty sandwiches. A long goods train with several carriages behind can look spectacular. Just build up a multi-layered sandwich for the steam engine with a chunk of celery for a funnel and sliced peppers for the wheels. Following behind could be single-layered sandwiches with small chunks of cheese, cucumber and tomato and thinly sliced radishes for the wheels. Add a railway track made from crossed twiglets and you are all set.

How about traffic-light sandwiches; simply trim off the crusts, cut the bread in half and spread with butter or cream cheese. Put a slice of tomato at the top, a slice of hard-boiled egg in the middle and a slice of cucumber at the bottom.

Another idea is to cut out circles of bread using round metal cutters and make open sandwiches that look like faces. Spread with a smooth filling or cut out a round piece of cheese, use grated carrot or salad cress for the hair, sliced grape or carrot for the eyes, sliced mushroom for the nose and a sliver of red pepper for the mouth.

Please note: If using a Circotherm oven (fan oven) for baking, the oven temperature should be reduced accordingly (see below).

CONVENTIONAL	CIRCOTHERM
160°C	150°C
180–190°C	160°C
200°C	170°C

patchwork quilt N

This is an attractive way of displaying miniature sandwiches – choose toppings of contrasting colours. There are lots of different foods you can use for decoration. This looks great for a special tea party and children will be able to choose their favourite sandwich from the patchwork quilt – ask them if they know what each sandwich is made from! Alternatively, you can make a patchwork quilt on one slice of bread (see illustration). Cut contrasting coloured cheese slices (e.g. Double Gloucester and Edam) into squares. Arrange like a chess board on top of the bread and decorate.

4 pieces wholemeal bread
Butter or margarine for spreading
A variety of different toppings – peanut butter, Marmite, different coloured

cheeses, egg mayonnaise, etc.
Grapes, sliced cherry tomatoes, cucumber, radishes, salad cress, etc. for decoration

Spread the slices of bread with butter or margarine. Remove the crusts and cut each slice into strips. Put a different topping on each strip and then cut each strip into small squares from each slice of bread. On a large plate, arrange the small squares in rows, mixing up the different toppings, to make one large square. Decorate some of the squares.

makes 36 miniature open sandwiches

tractor sandwich

This makes a great centrepiece for a birthday party and never fails to impress (see the illustration). Simply layer brown and white bread and spread with different but complementary fillings like egg and cress, cream cheese, cucumber, tomato and so on and form into the shape of a tractor. Make the trailer from one and a half bagels, and line up some fresh farm produce like cherry tomatoes, cucumber and celery. Make the wheels from sliced red peppers and carrot slices, the windows from cheese slices and chives and a sesame stick for the funnel. The children will have a great time taking it to pieces!

multi-layered sandwiches

Layer 3 or 4 slices of bread together with 1 or 2 different fillings. Use brown or white bread or mix them together. Cut the bread into fingers, small squares or miniature triangles. Make sure the 2 fillings are complementary!

pinwheel sandwiches

These are fun to make and can be frozen in long rolls before they are sliced, wrapped in cling film. Use a denser bread and if you can chill it first this will make it easier to handle. Remove the crusts from 2 slices of bread, lay them on a board so that the edges overlap by about 1 cm (1/2 inch). Flatten them so that the bread becomes pliable and the 2 pieces are firmly joined together. Butter the bread and spread with your desired filling. Fillings which contrast with the colour of the bread look best. Then carefully roll up the bread along its longest edge. Below is a list of suggested fillings that work well with pinwheel sandwiches.

peanut butter **N**

peanut butter and jam **N**

smooth egg mayonnaise with snipped chives or mustard and cress

smoked salmon

salmon mousse

chopped spinach, cream cheese, finely grated Parmesan and a little nutmeg

Peanut Alert: peanuts can cause allergic reactions (see page 18).

toasted sandwiches

Miniature toasted sandwiches are very tempting. Cook the open sandwiches under a hot grill for about 5 minutes. Below are some suggested toppings for you to try.

cheese, tomato and snipped chives

home-made pizza topping – chopped and sautéed tomato, spring onion and mushroom with some sliced Bel Paese or Mozzarella cheese on top

cooked chopped chicken with sautéed mushrooms in a béchamel sauce

sliced apple and banana, spinkled with some brown sugar and cinnamon

tuna, sweetcorn and melted cheese

more ideas for sandwiches and fillings

To stop the bread from going soggy, put lettuce leaves between the bread and the filling. Bread doesn't always need to be buttered – you can sometimes use fromage frais, curd or cream cheese or peanut butter instead.

mashed avocado and cream cheese

chopped chicken or turkey with fruit chutney

peanut butter and raspberry jam **N**

peanut butter and mashed banana with alfalfa sprouts **N**

peanut butter and apple purée with raisins (and maybe a pinch of cinnamon) **N**

peanut butter, grated apple and toasted sesame seeds **N**

Cheddar cheese, Marmite and shredded lettuce

cream cheese, cucumber and toasted sesame seeds

chopped hard-boiled eggs, watercress or salad cress and mayonnaise

cream cheese and chopped, peeled grapes

cream cheese and crushed pineapple mashed sardine

natural fromage frais and raisins

grated cheese with grated apple and pear

tuna mayonnaise and salad cress or spring onion

tinned salmon, chopped egg and mayonnaise

raisin bread with cream cheese and strawberry jam

bagel with cream cheese and slices of smoked salmon

cottage cheese with ripe kiwi fruit slices

chopped chicken, mayonnaise and yoghurt with a little curry powder and raisins

prawns with shredded lettuce, tomato, cucumber and mayonnaise

grilled chicken liver mashed with fried onions and hard-boiled egg

egg mayonnaise with a 1/2 teaspoon of curry powder

cream cheese with chopped dates, prunes or dried apricots

cold chicken or turkey with avocado and tomato

cream cheese with fruit purée

chopped hard-boiled eggs with mashed sardines

grated Cheddar, carrot and mayonnaise

yummy jelly boats

These jelly boats are the most popular party food that I make. I usually make them using packets of fruit jelly, but you can also make them using fruit juices. Try cranberry and raspberry juice, tropical fruit juice, apple, grape or orange juice sweetened with a little sugar. Another idea is to make lime, peach and strawberry jelly in tall glasses and set them one after the other in three layers. You end up with traffic light jelly!

2 large oranges
1 x 11.7 g (approx. 1 tablespoon)
sachet gelatine

500 ml (16 fl oz) fruit juice
1 sheet of rice paper
8 cocktail sticks

Cut the oranges in half. Squeeze out the juice without breaking the skin and carefully scrape out the membrane and discard it (reserve the skins). Heat a little of the fruit juice in a saucepan, sprinkle over the gelatine and stir, making sure it dissolves completely. Stir in the rest of the fruit juice. Alternatively, use packet jelly and make up according to packet instructions.

   Fill each orange half with the jelly mixture and add some of the prepared fruit if you like. Make sure that the oranges are filled right to the top. Refrigerate until set and cut the oranges in half again (using a wet knife). Cut triangles out of the rice paper and secure with cocktail sticks to make sails.

makes 8 boats

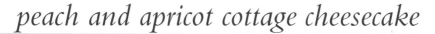

peach and apricot cottage cheesecake

This cake is simple to make, uses no cream, requires no baking and looks very impressive. A lovely cake to make for a special tea party. It also freezes very well so that you can make it in advance.

1 × 800-g (1 lb 12-oz) tin apricots
2 × 135-g (4 ¾-oz) packets peach jelly
750 g (1½ lb) cottage cheese
300 ml (10 fl oz) fromage frais
275 g (10 oz) ginger biscuits

75 g (3 oz) butter or margarine, melted
1 × 400-g (14-oz) tin apricots
3 tablespoons apricot jam, sieved
A little grated chocolate (optional)

Drain the large tin of apricots and reserve 8 tablespoons of syrup. Dissolve the jelly in this syrup in the top of a double boiler (or use an ordinary saucepan on top of a saucepan containing simmering water) and leave to cool. Put the cottage cheese through a mouli to make a smooth texture. Put the drained apricots into the mouli to make a purée and stir these into the cottage cheese. Stir in the cooled jelly mixture and the fromage frais.

Crush the ginger biscuits in a food processor and stir in the melted butter or margarine. Press the crushed biscuits onto the base of a 25-cm (10-inch) round cake tin and pour over the apricot cheese mixture.

Place the cake in a refrigerator until set and then decorate with the drained apricot halves from the remaining tin of apricots. Dissolve the apricot jam in 1 tablespoon of water and brush this glaze over the top of the cake. You can decorate the cake with a little grated chocolate if you wish.

makes 10 portions

mini party pizzas

These make popular party food and it is quite fun to let the children choose the toppings themselves before the pizzas are baked in the oven. It's also fun to decorate the pizzas by arranging the toppings to look like faces. As a quick alternative, you can use split muffins for the pizza bases.

250 g (8 oz) plain flour
½ teaspoon salt
1 egg yolk
3 tablespoons freshly grated Parmesan cheese
1 tablespoon fresh chopped parsley
3 tablespoons cold water
100 g (4 oz) butter

TOMATO SAUCE
1 small onion, finely chopped
1 clove garlic, crushed
2 tablespoons olive oil

1 x 400-g (14-oz) tin chopped tomatoes
2 tablespoons shredded basil leaves
½ teaspoon sugar
Salt and freshly ground black pepper

TOPPINGS
200 g (7 oz) Mozzarella cheese, diced
100 g (4 oz) Cheddar cheese, grated
Extra toppings: thinly sliced button mushrooms, tinned sweetcorn, diced peppers, sliced pepperami
Olive oil

Sift flour into a mixing bowl and add the Parmesan and parsley. Cut the butter into cubes and rub it into the flour mixture using your fingers. Mix in the egg yolk and water and knead the dough until smooth. Shape into a ball, wrap in cling film and chill in the fridge for 30 to 40 minutes. Roll out dough on a floured board until 12 cm (¼ inch) thick and cut into 8 mini pizzas using a 9-cm (3 ½-inch) plain pastry cutter.

While the dough is in the fridge, you can make the tomato sauce. Sauté the onion and garlic in the olive oil until softened, then stir in the chopped tomatoes, basil, sugar and seasonings. Cook over a medium heat until thickened (about 10 minutes).

Arrange the pizza bases on greased baking trays and spread each one with some of the tomato sauce. Divide the Mozzarella and Cheddar among the pizzas and add extra toppings of your choice. Drizzle over some olive oil and bake in an oven pre-heated to gas mark 6, 400°F (200°C) for 10 to 12 minutes or until the pastry is crisp and lightly golden.

makes 8 mini pizzas

crispy spring rolls

The most delicious Chinese vegetarian spring rolls filled with vegetables and rice noodles flavoured with soy sauce and served with a tasty dipping sauce. These are bound to be a great hit.

2 tablespoons vegetable oil
1 medium onion, sliced
1 clove garlic, crushed
75 g (3 oz) carrots, cut into thin strips
75 g (3 oz) red pepper, cut into thin strips
350 g (12 oz) Chinese cabbage, shredded
150 g (6 oz) beansprouts
250 g (8 oz) button mushrooms, sliced

2 spring onions, finely sliced
75 g (3 oz) fine rice noodles
1 tablespoon water
1 tablespoon cornflour
1 tablespoon oyster sauce
1/2 tablespoon soy sauce
1 teaspoon sugar
1 vegetable stock cube
24 spring roll wrappers
1 egg, beaten
Vegetable oil for deep frying

Heat the oil in a wok or frying pan and stir-fry the onion and garlic until lightly golden. Add the carrot and red pepper and stir-fry for 3 minutes.

Add the cabbage, beansprouts, mushrooms and spring onions and stir-fry for 3 to 4 minutes. Cook the rice noodles according to the instructions on the packet and then rinse in a colander under cold water. Cut the noodles into 2.5-cm (1-in) lengths. Stir the cornflour into the water and combine with the oyster sauce, soy sauce and sugar. Add the noodles to the vegetables in the wok, pour in the sauce and crumble over the stock cube. Stir-fry, mixing everything together, for 2 minutes.

Fold over one corner of each spring roll wrapper. Place 2 to 3 tablespoons of the filling about one-third of the way down. Roll over once, fold in both ends and roll over to form a spring roll. Brush the remaining corner with some beaten egg and press down to seal. To cook the spring rolls, heat the oil in a wok or deep fryer until hot, then reduce the heat. Deep fry the spring rolls in batches for 2 to 3 minutes or until lightly golden and crispy, then remove and drain. Serve the spring rolls hot with a dipping sauce, like the one below.

makes 24 spring rolls

dipping sauce for spring rolls

4 tablespoons rice wine vinegar
1 tablespoon soft brown sugar
4 tablespoons rice wine/sake
1 tablespoon soy sauce

1/4 red chilli, de-seeded and finely sliced
1 tablespoon finely sliced spring onion
(optional)
1/4 teaspoon grated root ginger (optional)

Place the vinegar and sugar in a pan and dissolve over a gentle heat. Bring to the boil and then simmer for 3 minutes until slightly reduced. Add the rice wine and bring to the boil, then remove from the heat and stir in the soy sauce. Allow to cool down a little and then stir in the chilli and spring onion (if using). If using ginger it should be added in the last minute of cooking the rice wine vinegar.

money bags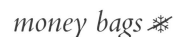

These little filo parcels are very attractive and much easier to make than they look. They can be made using a variety of different fillings like spinach and ricotta cheese, or use the spring roll mixture.

25 g (1 oz) butter
50 g (2 oz) finely chopped onion
50 g (2 oz) button mushrooms,
thinly sliced
25 g (1 oz) red pepper, diced
25 g (1 oz) green pepper, diced

50 g (2 oz) frozen sweetcorn
Salt and freshly ground black pepper
2 spring onions or 12 chives
12 small sheets of filo pastry 16 cm x
18 cm (6 inch x 8 inch)
Oil for frying

Melt the butter in a frying pan and sauté the onion and mushrooms for 3 minutes. Add the peppers and sweetcorn, season and cook for 4 minutes. Divide the filling into six portions.

Shred the spring onions and blanch in boiling water for 1 minute and then refresh in cold water.

Take two sheets of filo pastry, place one diagonally on top of the other so you form a star shape. Place a portion of filling in the centre. Gather all the corners together and tie with a strip of spring onion or a chive. Deep fry in hot oil for about 2 minutes or until golden.

makes 6 filo purses

fortune cookies ❄

These are great fun for parties or special occasions. My three children all play the violin and I often make these for all the performers after their concerts. I insert little messages like *You only need to practise on the days you eat* or *If only the best birds sang the woods would be silent.* Another idea is to write jokes on the strips of paper and insert these in the cookies.

50 g (2 oz) sugar	*50 g (2 oz) butter*
2 egg whites	*¼ teaspoon vanilla essence*
A pinch of salt	*50 g (2 oz) plain flour*

Pre-heat the oven to gas mark 4, 350°F (180°C). Write your message on small strips of paper. Beat the sugar into the egg whites with a fork and add the pinch of salt. Melt the butter and stir it into the eggs together with the vanilla. Gradually beat in the flour and mix until well blended. Drop teaspoonfuls of the batter onto greased baking sheets, making sure that they are spaced well apart. Bake in the oven for about 5 minutes or until the edges are lightly golden. The skill is to work quickly and mould the fortune cookies while they are still hot and pliable. Place a 'fortune' in the middle of each cookie and fold in half to form a semi-circle. Bend it again in the middle and weigh it down with a spoon or hold for a few seconds until it keeps its shape.

makes 16 fortune cookies

M&M cookies

Children love these cookies which are studded with brightly coloured candy-coated chocolates.

100 g (4 oz) brown sugar
75 g (3 oz) granulated sugar
25 g (1 oz) butter
15 g (½ oz) white vegetable shortening
1 teaspoon pure vanilla essence
1 egg

175 g (6 oz) plain flour
½ teaspoon baking soda
½ teaspoon salt
225 g (8 oz) candy-coated chocolate M&Ms

Heat the oven to gas mark 4, 350°F (180°C). Mix together the sugars, butter, shortening, vanilla and egg. Stir in the remaining ingredients. Drop heaped teaspoons of the dough spaced well apart onto ungreased cookie sheets. Bake for about 10 minutes until lightly golden. The centres will still be soft but will firm up later. Allow to cool down a little before removing from the cookie sheets.

makes approx. 35 cookies

quick and easy novelty-shape biscuits

These are always popular and are ideal for children to make themselves. There are lots of novelty biscuit cutters you can use to make attractive biscuits. You can decorate them with hundreds and thousands, chocolate vermicelli, edible silver balls or any other small cake decorations. You could also coat them with melted dark or white chocolate instead of coloured icing. To make chocolate biscuits, substitute 25 g (1 oz) of the flour with 25 g (1 oz) sifted cocoa .

100 g (4 oz) softened butter
50 g (2 oz) caster sugar
175 g (6 oz) plain flour
pinch of salt
a few drops of pure vanilla essence

ICING
100 g (4 oz) icing sugar, sifted
1 to 2 tablespoons freshly squeezed lemon juice
Assorted food colourings

Pre-heat the oven to gas mark 4, 350°F (180°C). Beat the butter and sugar together either by hand with a wooden spoon or in an electric mixer at low speed until thoroughly mixed. Sift together the flour and salt and mix this into the butter mixture together with a few drops of vanilla essence to form a fairly stiff dough. If the dough is too dry add a little water. Form the dough into a ball using your hands, then roll out thinly on a floured work surface using a rolling pin dusted with flour. Cut into novelty shapes using biscuit cutters. Collect all the trimmings together and roll these out again to make more biscuits. Add any edible silver balls or currants needed, e.g. for 'eyes' before baking. Bake for about 15 minutes or until the biscuits are lightly golden.

To make the icing, put the icing sugar in a bowl and add enough lemon juice to make a good spreading consistency. Divide the icing into two or three small bowls and add a drop of different colouring to each bowl, stirring until combined. Spread the icing onto the cooled biscuits with a small palette knife or back of a teaspoon.

makes approx. 35 cookies

scrumptious marble cake squares

This not only looks fabulous but tastes great too! It never lasts long in my house.

75 g (3 oz) plain chocolate
175 g (6 oz) unsalted butter
50 g (2 oz) white chocolate
4 eggs
250 g (9 oz) soft light brown sugar
175 g (6 oz) plain flour, sifted

1 x 142 ml (5 fl oz) carton sour cream

CHOCOLATE SATIN GLAZE
75 g (3 oz) semi-sweet chocolate
25 g (1 oz) butter
50 g (2 oz) white chocolate

Pre-heat the oven to gas mark 3, 325°F (160°C). Put the plain chocolate and half the butter in a covered microwave dish and cook on full power for 1½ minutes, stirring halfway through. Alternatively gently heat the chocolate and butter in a saucepan until melted. Set aside to cool. Melt the remaining butter together with the white chocolate and set aside to cool.

Beat the eggs and sugar together in an electric mixer for 5 minutes until light and fluffy. Transfer half the mixture to another bowl. Stir the plain chocolate mixture into one bowl and the white chocolate mixture into the other. Fold half the flour and half the sour cream into each.

Place alternate tablespoons of the mixture into a lined 28 cm x 18-cm (11 x 7-inch) shallow baking tin. Swirl the mixture with a blunt knife to create a marbled effect and bake in the oven for 30 to 35 minutes.

To make the glaze melt the semi-sweet chocolate and butter together in a microwave for 1½ minutes on full power, stirring halfway through. Alternatively melt in a double boiler, stirring until smooth.

Once the cake has cooled down, spread the glaze over the top. Melt the white chocolate and using a teaspoon trail 5 lines horizontally across the cake about 2½ cm (1 inch) apart. With a skewer or blunt knife draw vertical lines lightly through the chocolate topping to create a pattern. Allow to cool

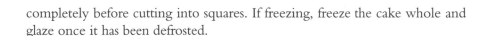

completely before cutting into squares. If freezing, freeze the cake whole and glaze once it has been defrosted.

makes 15 squares

chocolate and apricot Rice Crispie squares

These are quite delicious and very popular. They are also a good recipe for children to make themselves as they are easy to prepare.

150 g (5 oz) rolled oats
50 g (2 oz) Rice Crispies
50 g (2 oz) chocolate chips

100 g (4 oz) chopped dried apricots
100 g (4 oz) unsalted butter
175 g (6 oz) golden syrup

Combine the oats, Rice Crispies, chocolate chips and dried apricots in a mixing bowl. Put the butter and the syrup in a saucepan and heat gently, stirring until melted. A handy tip for measuring the amount of syrup needed is first to weigh the whole tin and then spoon out as much syrup as necessary to decrease the weight by 175 g (6 oz). Stir the butter and syrup mixture into the dry ingredients until well coated. Press the mixture into a 28 x 18 cm (11 x 7 inch) shallow tin and store in the fridge. Cut into squares and keep these in the fridge until ready to serve.

makes 15 squares

best-ever brownies

Children love brownies but prefer them without chopped nuts so I have added white and dark chocolate chips and the zest of an orange to give these a luxurious flavour. They have a rich moist taste that will have you coming back for more. These brownies will keep for at least a week in a sealed container.

125 g (4½ oz) good quality plain chocolate broken into pieces
175 g (6 oz) unsalted butter
4 eggs
75 g (3 oz) caster sugar
75 g (3 oz) light muscovado sugar
Finely grated zest of one orange (about 1 teaspoon)

75 g (3 oz) ground almonds
75 g (3 oz) plain flour
50 g (2 oz) plain chocolate chips
50 g (2 oz) white chocolate chips
Sifted icing sugar

Pre-heat the oven to gas mark 4, 350°F (180°C). Melt the chocolate and butter together in a suitable covered dish either in the microwave for 2 minutes or in a bowl over a saucepan of simmering water. Whisk the eggs, sugars and orange zest in an electric mixer for about 5 minutes or until light and fluffy. Stir in the melted chocolate mixture. Fold in the ground almonds, flour and chocolate chips. Grease and line a 20-cm (8-inch) square tin and pour the mixture into the tin. Bake for about 30 minutes or until well risen and slightly firm at the edges. Leave to cool in the tin, then turn out, dust the top with sifted icing sugar and cut into small squares.

makes 16 squares

butterfly cakes

These are a variation on traditional fairy cakes but with a circle of cut-out cake sliced in half and replaced on top of the cake to look like the wings of a butterfly. You can really go to town on the decoration if you like. You can decorate the wings using coloured tubes of writing icing, you can pipe the whipped cream and sprinkle over some hundreds and thousands or scatter over a few edible silver balls.

100 g (4 oz) soft margarine
100 g (4 oz) caster sugar
2 eggs
100 g (4 oz) self-raising flour
1 teaspoon pure vanilla essence
strawberry jam

300 ml (10 fl oz) double cream,
whipped
icing sugar
Edible silver balls or hundreds and
thousands

Pre-heat the oven to gas mark 4, 350°F (180°C). Beat the margarine and sugar together until light and fluffy. Mix in the eggs, one at a time together with 1 tablespoon of the flour, then beat in the vanilla essence and the remaining flour. Put 12 paper cases into a bun tin and bake the cakes for about 20 minutes, then put them on a wire rack to cool.

Using a fine pointed knife, cut circles from the top of the cakes about 1 cm (⅓ inch) in from the edge and about 1½ cm (½ inch) deep. Cut these circles in half. Place a teaspoon of jam in the hollow of the cake and add a swirl of whipped cream. Place the two half slices of the cake butterfly fashion on top of the cream and dust with a little sifted icing sugar. Add extra decorations if you like.

makes 12 cakes

HALLOWEEN

pumpkin soup

For Halloween, Cinderella's pumpkin (see page 36) can be magically transformed into a delicious soup for the family. Simply increase the quantities in the recipe and add extra stock. You can spice up the soup by adding some fresh chopped ginger. For an impressive serving idea pour the soup into a hollowed-out pumpkin shell.

spooky ghost cakes

Dariole or timbale moulds are the ideal shape for these spooky little cakes.

100 g (4 oz) soft margarine
100 g (4 oz) caster sugar
1 teaspoon finely grated lemon rind
100 g (4 oz) self-raising flour
1 teaspoon baking powder

2 eggs
1 teaspoon pure vanilla essence
450 g (1 lb) white ready-to-roll icing
1 tube of black writing icing
2 strips of liquorice

Pre-heat the oven to gas mark 4, 350°F (180°C). Cream the margarine and sugar together with the lemon rind until light and fluffy. Sift together the flour and baking powder. Beat in the eggs one at a time with the vanilla essence, adding 1 tablespoon flour mixture for each egg. Fold in the remaining flour. Bake in greased dariole or timbale moulds for 20 to 25 minutes. Turn out the cakes and leave to cool on a wire rack. Take about 75 g (3 oz) icing at a time and roll this out thinly on a clean work surface dusted with icing sugar to make circles of icing about 18 cm (7 inch) in diameter. Drape these over the cakes and draw eyes and nose with black writing icing and use a small strip of black liquorice for the mouth.

makes about 6 ghost cakes

pumpkin oranges ✳

These oranges are cut out to look like mini pumpkins and then filled with a selection of cut up fruits or chopped jelly.

Cut a slice from the stalk end of each orange and hollow out using a small sharp knife and teaspoon. Cut out eyes, nose and mouth shapes from the shell and cut a small sliver from the base of the orange so that it stands upright.

dead man's fingers

These goulish sandwiches look terrific!

Thin sliced white bread, crusts removed
A little soft margarine
Cream cheese or peanut butter

Flaked almonds
Strawberry jam

Gently flatten the slices of bread with a rolling pin to make them more pliable. Spread with a little margarine and either some cream cheese or peanut butter. Roll up the sandwiches and make three indentations with a blunt knife to form the finger joints. Stick the flaked almonds on the tips with a little cream cheese or peanut butter to form the nails and some strawberry jam for the blood!

wicked witches' ice-cream N

Transform an upside-down ice-cream cone over a scoop of ice-cream into a wicked witch. I particularly like to use pistachio ice-cream which gives the witch a green face.

Ice-cream, vanilla, pistachio or strawberry
Ice-cream cones

DECORATION
Red, black or green liquorice laces for the hair
Green or red glacé cherries for the eyes
Large jelly beans for the nose
Red liquorice for the mouth

Put two scoops of ice-cream one on top of each other on plastic or paper plates and put in the freezer to set. Meanwhile, mix up some icing sugar with a little water to form a sticky paste and use this to attach strands of liquorice to the inside rim of the ice-cream cones to form the witches' hair. Decorate the top scoop of ice-cream to look like the face of a witch.

hot potato witches ❄

A fun way to jolly up a baked potato! If you like you can remove the flesh from the potato leaving the skin intact, then mash the potato together with some butter, milk and seasoning and stuff it back inside the potato.

2 medium, round baking potatoes
A little vegetable oil
2 sheets black paper
1 small bunch of chives

2 stuffed olives
2 baby carrots
1 strip of red pepper
Cream cheese, for 'glue'

Wash and dry the potatoes, prick all over with a fork and brush with oil. Bake in a hot oven for between 1 hour and 1 hour 15 minutes, until tender (alternatively cook in a microwave/grill combination for about 15 minutes, turning halfway through). Make little witches' hats by cutting circles from the black paper and rolling into a cone. Place the chives in the microwave for 8 to 10 seconds – this will make them more pliable and you will be able to stick them on top of the potato to make the witches' green hair. Decorate the potatoes to look like witches' faces with slices of stuffed olives for the eyes, the tip of the baby carrot for a nose and a strip of red pepper for the mouth. These can be attached to the potato with a dab of cream cheese. Place the black hats on the witches' heads.

makes 2 portions

witches' broomsticks ❄

If you find it too fiddly to use chives to tie the Twiglets to the broomstick,
you could use a strip of liquorice instead.

6 twisted cheese straws   *6 chives or strips of spring onion*
1 packet Twiglets

Simply attach 4 Twiglets onto the end of each cheese straw by tying them
on with a knotted chive or strip of spring onion.

makes 6 broomsticks

black cat biscuits

Make the recipe for *quick and easy novelty biscuits* or *teddy bear biscuits* and make
up a quantity of black icing made with icing sugar, lemon juice and black food
colouring (see page 153 or 161). Use edible silver balls for the cat's eyes.

A Teddy Bear's Picnic

It's worth looking out for teddy bear cutters and teddy bear moulds when you are in a department store or kitchen shop. Cookie cutters can be used to make sandwiches as well as biscuits and it's surprising what novely shapes can do to stimulate your child's appetite.

I found recently some mini tedd bear moulds which are terrific fo making small sponge cakes and jellies.

little miss muffin **N**

Children love dainty food and miniature muffins are very appealing. The carrot and pineapple muffin recipe on page 136 is ideal for making into mini muffins. Chop up the raisins and leave out the pecans if your child prefers these without nuts. Bake in mini muffin trays lined with paper cases and bake for about 20 minutes at gas mark 4, 350°F (180°C).

teddy bear sandwiches **N** ❄

It's fun to make peanut butter sandwiches cut into teddy bear shapes using currants for eyes.

teddy bear biscuits

Little children love cut-out biscuits and these are easy and quick to make. I have various size teddy bear biscuit cutters so I can make a whole family of teddy bears. They look great if you tie thin ribbons around their necks. If you can't find edible silver balls use currants or blobs of writing icing (available in tubes in supermarkets). These biscuits could also be covered with melted chocolate if you like.

100 g (4 oz) butter, softened
225 g (8 oz) self-raising flour
¼ teaspoon salt
100 g (4 oz) caster sugar
¼ teaspoon vanilla essence
½ egg, beaten (about 3 tablespoons)

1 tablespoon milk

DECORATION
Edible silver balls
Thin ribbon

Pre-heat the oven to gas mark 4, 350°F (180°C). Rub the butter into the flour with your fingers until the mixture resembles fine breadcrumbs. Mix in the salt, sugar, vanilla essence, beaten egg and milk to form a ball of fairly stiff dough. Roll out the dough on a floured work surface until quite thin and cut into teddy bear shapes using biscuit cutters. Gather up any scraps of dough and roll them out again. Arrange two edible silver balls on the teddy bears' faces to form the eyes.

Place the teddy bears on greased baking trays and bake for about 10 minutes or until golden. Cool on a wire rack. Tie bows of ribbon round the teddy bears' necks if you like.

makes about 30 teddy bears

chocolate teddy bear cakes

I make these individual chocolate cakes in teddy bear moulds which are 11 cm (4 ½ inch) high. These are fun for children to make and decorate themselves. You can also use the sponge mixture for the *spooky ghost cakes* to make mini teddy bear cakes.

2 tablespoons cocoa
2 tablespoons hot water
175 g (6 oz) soft margarine
175 g (6 oz) caster sugar
3 eggs
150 g (5 oz) self-raising flour
1 teaspoon baking powder

1 teaspoon vanilla essence

DECORATION
Smarties, red liquorice laces, edible silver balls, Jelly Tots, chocolate chips, tubes of writing icing

Blend the cocoa with the hot water in a small bowl and set aside. Cream the margarine and sugar together until fluffy. Sift together the flour and baking powder. Beat in the eggs one at a time with a spoonful of the flour mixture. Mix in the remaining flour, cocoa and the vanilla essence. Grease the teddy bear moulds and spoon the mixture into the moulds until about two-thirds full. Bake in the oven for about 25 minutes or until a skewer inserted in the centre comes out clean.

makes about 8 chocolate teddy bear cakes

teddy bear fairy cakes

It's easy to turn fairy cakes into something special.

100 g (4 oz) soft margarine
100 g (4 oz) caster sugar
1 teaspoon pure vanilla essence
2 eggs
100 g (4 oz) self-raising flour
1 teaspoon grated lemon rind
1 tablespoon hot water

50 g (2 oz) raisins (optional)

DECORATION
Chocolate buttons, Smarties, Jelly Tots,
a Tube of black writing icing and a little
icing sugar

Pre-heat the oven to gas mark 4, 350°F (180°C). Cream the margarine and sugar together with the lemon rind until light and fluffy, then beat in the eggs one at a time together with 1 tablespoon of the flour. Add the vanilla. Fold in the remaining flour, hot water and raisins, if using. Line a bun or muffin tray with paper cases and half fill each case with the mixture. Bake in the oven for about 15 minutes.

Mix together a few tablespoons of icing sugar with cold water to make a sticky paste and use this to stick the Smarties, chocolate buttons and Jelly Tots onto the cakes to look like the teddy's eyes, ears and nose. Add a mouth using the black writing icing.

makes 12 teddy bear cakes

CHRISTMAS

Christmas tree biscuits

It's fun to make biscuits to hang on the Christmas tree. Simply make a hole near the top of these biscuits with a sharp skewer while the biscuits are still warm from the oven. Once you have decorated the biscuits you can thread some thin tartan ribbon through the holes and tie the biscuits onto the branches. Some biscuits can be iced bright colours and decorated with silver or sugar-coated balls and others can be left plain and decorated with writing icing.

50 g (2 oz) butter
100 g (4 oz) soft brown sugar
4 tablespoons golden syrup
225g (8 oz) plain flour
Pinch of salt
1 teaspoon bicarbonate of soda
1 teaspoon ground ginger
1 teaspoon ground cinnamon

1 egg yolk, lightly beaten
2 teaspoons milk

ICING
100 g (4 oz) icing sugar, sieved
About 1 tablespoon lemon juice
Food colouring (red, green, yellow)

Put the butter, brown sugar and golden syrup in a saucepan and heat gently, stirring until melted. Set aside to cool. Sift together the flour, bicarbonate of soda, ginger and cinnamon. Mix the butter and syrup mixture into the flour together with the beaten egg yolk and milk to make a firm dough. Wrap in cling film and chill in the fridge for 30 minutes. Sift some icing sugar onto a clean work surface and roll out the dough to a ½ cm (¼ inch) thickness. Cut into shapes using a variety of Christmas cookie cutters. Press some silver or coloured balls into the biscuits to decorate them if you like. Arrange on greased baking sheets and bake in an oven pre-heated to gas mark 4, 350°F (180°C) for about 10 minutes or until firm. If you want to use these biscuits to decorate a Christmas tree, make small holes near the top of the biscuits using a skewer while the biscuits are still warm. Transfer to a wire rack to cool. Put the icing sugar in a bowl and add enough lemon juice to make a good spreading consistency. Divide the icing into two bowls and add a few drops of different coloured icing to each bowl. Decorate the biscuits with piped icing or silver balls and thread tartan ribbon through the holes if using them as Christmas tree decorations.

makes about 25 biscuits

baby Christmas puddings

Children like the look of Christmas puddings but often don't like the taste. These miniature Christmas puddings look fantastic and children love eating them too! They are also fun for children to make themselves with a little adult supervision.

200 g (7 oz) plain chocolate
50 g (2 oz) butter
2 tablespoons golden syrup
225 g (8 oz) digestive biscuits
50 g (2 oz) dried apricots,
finely chopped
50 g (2 oz) golden sultanas
50 g (2 oz) raisins

50 g (2 oz) glacé cherries, chopped
75 g (3 oz) ready-to-roll white icing
Icing sugar for dusting
1 tablespoon apricot jam
50 g (2 oz) green ready-to-roll icing
Edible sugar-coated red balls or use
25 g (1 oz) ready-to-roll red icing

Melt the chocolate together with the butter and golden syrup in a saucepan over a low heat, stirring occasionally for about 4 minutes (or in a microwave for about 2 minutes, stirring halfway through). Put the biscuits into a plastic bag and crush into very small pieces with a rolling pin. Mix the biscuits into the melted chocolate mixture together with the dried fruit and glacé cherries. Set aside to cool in the fridge for about 30 minutes. Using your hands, roll tablespoons of the mixture into about 20 balls. Dust a clean work surface lightly with icing sugar and roll out the white icing until quite thin. Use a small petal shape cutter or cut small circular wavy shapes with a sharp knife by hand from the icing. Brush the tops of the puddings with a little warmed apricot jam and stick the circles of icing on top. Roll out the green icing until quite thin and cut out some holly leaves using a small cutter. If you can't find ready-made green icing, you can make your own by kneading white icing with a few drops of green food colouring. Use tiny red sugar-coated balls for the berries or roll a little red icing to make tiny red balls. Attach the decorations to the puddings with a little apricot jam.

<u>*makes about 20*</u>

Christmas cake

This cake matures if kept so I make several of these cakes 3 to 4 weeks before Christmas as they make wonderful Christmas presents for your children's teachers of friends. I put them on round cake boards, decorate the tops with holly and glacé fruits and them put them into fancy cake tins. I fill the gap around the edge of the cake tin with some shredded red tissue paper.

350 g (12 oz) raisins	*4 tablespoons brandy*
275 g (10 oz) sultanas	*4 tablespoons port*
275 g (10 oz) currants	*250 g (9 oz) butter, softened*

250 g (9 oz) dark muscovado sugar
350 g (12 oz) plain flour
1 teaspoon baking powder
pinch of salt
6 eggs
50 g (2 oz) ground almonds

1 teaspoon mixed spice
1 teaspoon cinnamon
1 teaspoon grated lemon rind
50 g (2 oz) mixed peel
100 g (4 oz) glacé cherries, halved
50 g (2 oz) blanched almonds, chopped

Put the raisins, sultanas and currants in a large bowl and pour in the brandy and port. Leave to soak overnight. Next day, line and grease a 23-cm (9-inch) round cake tin. Tie a double thickness of brown paper around the outside of the cake tin to come up about 4 cm (1½ inch) higher than the cake. This will prevent the edges of the cake becoming brown and overcooked before the inside is cooked through. Pre-heat the oven to gas mark 2, 300°F (150°C). Beat the butter and sugar together until fluffy. Sift together the flour, baking powder and salt. Beat in the eggs one at a time adding 1 tablespoon of the flour mixture with each of the eggs. Beat in the remaining flour and the ground almonds. Add the mixed spice, cinnamon and lemon rind. Finally mix in the dried fruits, mixed peel, glacé cherries and nuts. Spoon the mixture into the tin and level the surface. Bake in the centre of the oven for 2½ hours or until the cake is firm to the touch and a skewer in the centre comes out clean. After 1 hour, check to see whether the cake is getting too brown. If it is, cover it with some greaseproof paper. Remove from the oven and leave to cool in the tin for about 30 minutes. Turn out onto a wire rack and cool. Wrap tightly in foil and store in a cool dry place. The cake can be left plain or can be covered with a thin layer of marzipan and white icing and then decorated.

snowballs of ice-cream

Simply roll scoops of ice-cream in grated white chocolate and return to the freezer to set.

fairy princess cake **N**

This is not a difficult cake to make but it looks quite spectacular. My friend Nicky Mallows, who is an artist, made up this cake for her daughter Laura's fourth birthday. My daughter Scarlet was so taken with the cake that she wanted exactly the same for her birthday, and no other cake would do! So Nicky showed me how she made it and now I will share that recipe with you to make every little girl's dream come true. You can make the cake ahead and pop it in the freezer before decorating if you wish.

175 g (5 oz) butter, softened
150 g (5 oz) soft margarine
275 g (10 oz) caster sugar (or use
275 g (10 oz) vanilla sugar and leave
out the vanilla essence)
6 eggs
225 g (8 oz) self-raising flour
1/2 teaspoon baking powder
Pinch of salt
100 g (4 oz) ground almonds
1 teaspoon vanilla essence
1 teaspoon almond essence

for the buttercream
175 g (6 oz) unsalted butter, softened
250 g (9 oz) sifted icing sugar
Grated rind of 2 lemons

for decoration
6 tablespoons apricot jam
500 g (18 oz) golden marzipan
1 large box (1 kg, 2 lb 3 oz) white
ready-to-roll icing
1 egg white
200 g (7 oz) icing sugar plus extra for
rolling
A little lemon juice
8 ready-made pink iced roses
Pink food colouring
Multi-coloured iced gem biscuits
Edible gold or silver balls
White and pink marshmallows
1 feather
1 small doll
1 pink Party Ring iced biscuit
1 paper umbrella

Pre-heat the oven to gas mark 4, 350°F (180°C). Beat the butter, margarine and sugar together until light and fluffy. Beat in the eggs one at a time together with 1 tablespoon flour to stop the mixture curdling. Mix in the remaining flour, baking powder and salt. Fold in the ground almonds, vanilla and almond essence until thoroughly blended. Pour the mixture into a greased and floured 1.2-litre (2-pint), 17-cm (6 ½-inch) diameter pudding basin and a 20–cm (8-inch) ring mould. Bake for 20 minutes, then reduce the heat to gas mark 3, 325°F, 160°C and bake for a further 25 minutes for the ring mould and about 40 minutes for the pudding basin (test with a skewer to make sure the cake is cooked). The ring mould will take less time to cook than the pudding basin and will need to be removed from the oven first.

Allow the cakes to cool on a wire rack. Meanwhile prepare the buttercream. Cream the butter and sifted icing sugar in an electric mixer (or use a bowl and wooden spoon), then beat in the grated lemon rind. Cut the pudding basin cake horizontally into three sections and the one from the ring mould horizontally in half. Sandwich these layers together with the buttercream icing. Gently warm the apricot jam either in a saucepan or in the microwave. Brush the ring mould cake with a little warm apricot jam and place the pudding basin sponge on top. Brush the entire surface of the cake with half the apricot jam. Roll out the marzipan on a cling-film covered work surface lightly dusted with icing sugar to form a large circle big enough to cover the cake. (The marzipan will be much easier to handle if it is rolled out on top of cling film or a plastic bag.) Lift the marzipan with the aid of the cling film and using your rolling pin as support, drape it over the cake. Smooth the marzipan into position with the palm of your hand working from the centre to the edge and down the sides. Trim away any excess marzipan with a sharp knife. Use the remaining apricot jam to brush over the marzipan to ensure that the icing sticks to the cake. Roll out about 750 g (1 lb 10 oz) of the icing to form a large circle about 45 cm (18 inch) diameter – again this is best done on top of cling film. Cut the circumference of the circle in a fairly free wavy pattern. Drape the icing over the cake so that it is smooth at the top but then hangs down in folds to form the skirt.

To make up the icing to pipe around the dress, beat a small egg white until stiff then gently beat in about 200 g (7 oz) icing sugar with a squeeze of lemon to get a fairly stiff mixture. Pipe this icing in two layers around the dress to form the ruching and decorate with the pink roses. Take some of the remaining ready-to-roll icing and knead thoroughly with a few drops of pink food colouring to make an even pale pink icing. Roll this out thinly onto a surface dredged with sifted icing sugar and cut into decorative shapes like hearts and diamonds using small cookie cutters. Remove the pink and white swirls of icing from the gem biscuits. Decorate the cake with the pink cut-out icing shapes, edible gold balls, swirls of pink and white icing from the gem biscuits and mini marshmallows as in the illustration. Using a sharp knife cut a hole in the centre of the cake, removing the inside and place the doll (appropriately dressed) in the centre of the cake.

To add the finishing touch, make a hat by attaching a pink Party Ring biscuit at a jaunty angle on the doll's head with a little of the piped icing, place an iced gem biscuit in the centre and decorate with a feather. You can add edible gold balls for earings and give the doll an umbrella to hold.

fairy tale castle cake

This birthday cake only needs assembling and decorating since it is made with bought madeira cakes and Swiss rolls. It looks fabulous and if you follow the instructions carefully you can't go wrong

3 madeira cakes
2 large and 1 small Swiss roll
5 tablespoons apricot jam
6 ice-cream cones

PINK BUTTER ICING
225 g (8 oz) unsalted butter
450 g (1 lb) sifted icing sugar
7 teaspoons milk
A few drops of pink food colouring

WHITE ICING
100 g (4 oz) unsalted butter
225 g (8 oz) sifted icing sugar
4 teaspoons milk

WHITE ROYAL ICING
1 large egg white
200 g (7 oz) icing sugar
or buy a tube of decorating icing

DECORATION
Coloured mini marshmallows
Iced gem biscuits
Ice-cream wafers for windows
3 pink wafer sandwiches for drawbridge
Matchmaker chocolates for portcullis
75 g (3 oz) desiccated coconut
A few drops of blue food colouring

Trim the madeira cakes if necessary so that you end up with a level block. Warm and sieve the apricot jam. Stick the madeira cakes in the centre of a 32-cm (12½-inch) square cake board by brushing the base of the cakes with a little of the apricot jam. Cream the butter and icing sugar together and beat in the milk and pink food colouring to make a pink butter icing of spreading consistency. Cover the surface of the cake with pink butter icing and smooth evenly with a palette knife. Cut each of the Swiss rolls in half and cover the sides of these with the pink butter icing. Place the two smaller Swiss roll halves on top of the madeira cake in the front two corners and place two of the large halves on the two back corners. Place the two remaining large halves on either side of the castle at the back and secure them to the cake board with a little apricot jam. Cream the butter, icing sugar and milk together to make a white icing of spreading consistency.

Cover the 6 ice-cream cones with the white icing using a palette knife. Attach the cones to form turrets, either using some icing or if you want the castle to be more secure, stick a fairly long bamboo skewer through each of the Swiss rolls and rest the ice-cream cones on these.

Cut the wafers carefully with a serrated edge knife to make the windows of the castle and press these onto the Swiss rolls. Decorate the turrets with mini marshmallows and the base of the castle with iced gem biscuits. Make a drawbridge from 2½ pink wafer sandwiches and cut some Matchmakers down to size to form the portcullis. To make the white royal icing for piping the windows, beat the egg white and gradually add it to the sifted icing sugar beating until the icing is smooth (add more or less icing sugar to make the right consistency for piping). Alternatively, you can buy tubes of decorating icing with piping nozzles to save time. Using a small star nozzle, pipe little rosettes around the wafer windows and decorate the drawbridge. To create the moat around the castle, mix the desiccated coconut with a few drops of the blue food colouring and a few drops of water. Brush the cake board with some warm, sieved apricot jam and strew the coconut over the cake board.

chocolate choo choo

This is one the simplest birthday cakes to make but also one of the most popular. The beauty of this cake is that there is no cooking required. All you have to do is assemble the ingredients and your child will love giving you a helping hand! This makes a great centrepiece if placed down the middle of a long table (see page 2).

CHOCOLATE ICING
100 g (4 oz) unsalted butter, softened
225 g (8 oz) sifted icing sugar
1 tablespoon sieved cocoa

8 long Matchmaker chocolate sticks
(1 x 120 g, 4 ¼ oz box)
1 x 150 g (5 oz) box milk chocolate

fingers
1 x 150 g (5 oz) box plain chocolate fingers
100 g (4 oz) milk chocolate for melting
4 x 205 g (7 ¼ oz) milk-chocolate-coated Swiss rolls
14 mini milk-chocolate Swiss rolls

DECORATION
1 chocolate marshmallow tea cake
1 chocolate Rolo
6 iced Party Ring biscuits
1 liquorice Catherine wheel

Liquorice Allsorts
Smarties
Dolly Mixture
Jelly Beans

Fix two cake boards together to form a long narrow board approximately 90 x 18 cm (36 x 7 inches). Make the chocolate icing by beating the butter, icing sugar and cocoa together. Spread most of the icing over the cake board, keeping a little in reserve. To make the track, lay two parallel lines of 4 Matchmakers end to end about 6 cm (2½ inches) apart. Lay milk and plain chocolate fingers alternately across the track to form the railway line. To secure the chocolate fingers to the track it's a good idea to heat a palette knife over a gas flame and gently rub it under the ends of the chocolate fingers so that the chocolate melts a little and ensures that the chocolate fingers stick to the Matchmakers when attached. Put 7 mini chocolate rolls on the track to form the wheels of the engine, leaving the first Swiss roll uncovered to form the bumper. Lay one of the large chocolate rolls on top to form the engine. Melt the chocolate – this will act as a glue. Cut about 4 cm (1½ inches) off the end of one of the remaining large Swiss rolls and secure this on top of the engine with some melted chocolate or a cocktail stick to form the cab. Secure a marshmallow tea cake with a Rolo to form the chimney. Attach 3 Party Rings to each side of the engine to form the wheels and decorate the front with a liquorice Catherine wheel and two yellow liquorice sweets to form the buffers. Cut the remaining Swiss rolls in half to form the carriages of the train. Cut a thin slice off the top of each of the Swiss rolls to a make a flat surface and spread this thinly with the remaining chocolate buttercream. You should have 5 trucks, including the two-thirds remaining from the Swiss roll that was used to decorate the engine. Arrange the remaining mini Swiss rolls along the track to form the wheels and lay the trucks on top. Pile the sweets onto the open trucks.

Harry the hedgehog

It would be hard to find a cake tin the right shape for the body of a hedgehog so for this cake I use a (Duralex) heat-resistant glass salad bowl which is just the right shape – it is 20 cm (8 inches) in diameter 8 cm (3 ¼ inches) high and holds just over 1.2 litre (2 pints). If you don't have a suitable glass bowl, then an ovenproof 1.2 litres (2 pint) basin will do. This is a simple cake to make so it's also good for special tea parties when you want a fun cake for the children to eat.

175 g (6 oz) soft margarine
175 g (6 oz) caster sugar
3 eggs
150 g (5 oz) self-raising flour
1 teaspoon baking powder
25 g (1 oz) cocoa
1 tablespoon hot water

*D*ECORATION
50 g (2 oz) plain chocolate
125 g (4 ½ oz) unsalted butter, softened

175 g (6 oz) icing sugar, sieved

2 x 65 g (2 ½ oz) packets milk chocolate buttons
2 plain chocolate chips or raisins
1 glacé cherry
3 tablespoons apricot jam
65 g (2 ½ oz) desiccated coconut
A few drops of green food colouring
A few drops of water

Pre-heat the oven to gas mark 4, 350°F (180°C). Cream the margarine and sugar together until light and fluffy. Beat in the eggs, one at a time, adding 1 tablespoon flour with each egg. Sift together the remaining flour, baking powder and cocoa and fold this into the mixture together with the tablespoon of hot water. Grease the bowl or basin and spoon in the cake mixture. Bake in the oven for between 50 minutes and 1 hour. The cake is ready when a skewer inserted in the middle comes out clean. Allow the cake to cool a little then remove from the mould onto a wire rack.

To make the chocolate icing, break the chocolate into pieces and melt in a bowl over a pan of simmering water or in a microwave. Set aside to cool slightly. Beat the butter together with the icing sugar, then beat in the melted chocolate.

Cut the chocolate cake in half and sandwich the two halves together with a little of the chocolate icing. Spread the remaining icing over the surface of the cake. Place the cake in the centre a 25-cm (10-inch) cake board. Trim one edge of each chocolate button so that it is straight. This will make it easier to attach them to the cake. Arrange the buttons all over the cake, except for the front quarter, to form the prickles of the hedgehog. Gently rake the icing in the front with a fork to form the hedgehog's face and decorate with two plain chocolate chips or raisins for the eyes and a glacé cherry for the nose. Put the coconut into a bowl and mix with the green food colouring and water, stirring until it turns a light green colour. Brush the cake board with a thin layer of warmed apricot jam. Strew the coconut around the hedgehog on top of the jam (which will help it to stick) to give the hedgehog some grass to play on.

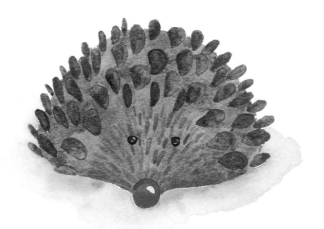

HEALTHY JUNK FOOD

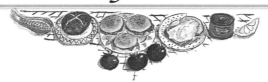

Kids love junk food but junk food doesn't love kids! If you ask children to name their favourite foods, chips, hamburgers and ice-cream would almost certainly come top of the list. Fast food companies are directly promoting their products at young children who are most in need of a diet rich in minerals and vitamins to fuel their growing bodies and children are faced with a limited range of foods, mainly highly processed and fried. Of course, the occasional visit to McDonalds will do your child no harm, and a dinner of fish fingers and chips when you have all had a busy day makes life nice and easy.

However, junk food on a regular basis is not a good idea. There is no law which obliges fast food companies to declare the ingredients of their products. Underneath the salt, monosodium glutamate, the colouring and the 'tasty' breadcrumbs and batters, often lurk inferior products like reconstituted fish or fatty minced meat. When it comes to dessert, manufacturers know that the sweeter the product the more it will appeal and the problem is that this intense sweetness becomes a learned habit and it can be hard to interest children in more natural, healthier foods.

A typical meal of hamburger, chips, apple pie and cola might well represent over 1200 calories, over two thirds of the daily calorie needs of a child between the ages of 4 and 6, and over half the daily calorie needs of an 11–14-year-old. However, this meal has a high proportion of saturated fat, salt and sugar but only a low level of nutrients for the calories provided. Growing consumption of junk food can lead to an increased incidence of heart disease, obesity and tooth decay and you may well end up with an overweight, unhappy child. The trouble is, we allow children choice before they have the ability to make informed decisions.

Not all 'junk' food is bad for you. Baked beans on toast make a great tea-time snack and some fish fingers and beefburgers are made with good quality ingredients. Give your child a healthier diet by following some of the tips below.

◆ When making chips, cut them thick to absorb less fat. Fry them in sunflower, safflower or corn oil and drain on kitchen paper before serving. Better still give a baked potato with an interesting topping.

◆ Grill beefburgers and choose a low-fat burger if possible and serve with a wholemeal bun.

◆ Choose wholemeal pizzas.

◆ Frozen vegetables, tinned fish and tinned beans are all good convenience foods to keep on hand.

◆ Buy tinned fruits in natural juices rather than sugary syrups.

◆ Choose dairy ice-creams made from good natural ingredients and make your own ice lollies from fruit juices (see page 115).

◆ Beware of many 'healthy' snacks like granola bars which are often laden with sugar – read the labels carefully.

There are lots of recipes in this section combining 'junk' food with other healthy ingredients to make complete meals, e.g. Minestrone with spaghetti hoops or Chicken nuggets with potato crisps. I have also made up my own healthy 'junk' food recipes for all time favourites like Pasta pizza and Funny face burgers to entice those junk food junkies back to Mum's home cooking!

minestrone with spaghetti hoops

Minestrone soup is very popular with children, they love to see all the 'bits' floating around. Combine it with a tin of spaghetti hoops and you are on to a real winner. You could try using the reduced-sugar spaghetti hoops now available.

2 onions, peeled and chopped
Vegetable oil for frying
1½ sticks celery, diced
2 carrots, peeled and grated
150 g (5 oz) shredded cabbage
3.4 litres (6 pints) chicken or vegetable stock (see pages 33–4)

2 tablespoons tomato purée
175 g (6 oz) frozen peas
1 large tin spaghetti hoops or spaghetti shapes
Salt and freshly ground black pepper
Grated Parmesan cheese to serve (optional)

Sauté the onions for 2 minutes in the oil then add the celery, carrots and cabbage and fry for a couple of minutes. In a separate pan, bring the stock to the boil and add the sautéed vegetables and tomato purée and simmer for about 10 minutes. Finally, add the peas and spaghetti hoops. Simmer for about 6 minutes, season with a little salt and pepper and serve. If you wish you can sprinkle some Parmesan cheese on top before serving.

makes about 12 portions

chicken nuggets with potato crisps

I make these with crushed cheese and onion crisps but you could try other flavours. Choose a good quality crisp without artificial flavours and colourings.

25 g (1 oz) cheese and onion crisps
1 slice of brown bread
1 egg
2 teaspoons water
Freshly ground black pepper

Flour for coating
1 large boneless chicken breast, cut into 8 pieces
Vegetable oil

Chop the bread and crisps in a food processor to the consistency of fine crumbs. Beat together the egg, water and black pepper in a shallow dish. Spread the flour in a second shallow dish and in a third dish, spread the mixture of crisps and breadcrumbs. Dip the chicken pieces first into the flour and then into the egg, letting the excess egg drip back into the dish. Finally, dip the chicken into the crumbs. Either sauté in oil for about 5 minutes or drizzle with a little oil and cook under a pre-heated grill for 10–15 minutes, or until cooked, turning halfway through.

makes 2 portions

pasta pizza ✳

Pizza with a spaghetti base – two favourites in one meal! Try this tasty cheese, mushroom and tomato topping and then add extra toppings that your child enjoys, like sweetcorn or salami, and you can have fun decorating them to look like faces.

175 g (6 oz) spaghetti
½ teaspoon salt
2 eggs, lightly beaten
120 ml (4 fl oz) milk
90 g (3 oz) Gruyère or Emmenthal
cheese, grated
25 g (1 oz) Cheddar cheese, grated
A little freshly ground black pepper
2 spring onions, chopped
10 button mushrooms, sliced

25 g (1 oz) butter or margarine
5 tomatoes, skinned, de-seeded and
chopped or 2 × 400-g (14-oz) tins
tomatoes, drained and chopped
50 ml (2 fl oz) tomato purée
1 tablespoon chopped basil
1 teaspoon oregano
100 g (4 oz) Mozzarella cheese, grated
25 g (1 oz) Parmesan cheese, grated
(optional)

Boil the pasta in salted water (leave a little undercooked as it will be cooked again in the oven). Drain and rinse under water. With a fork, beat together the eggs, milk and 40 g (1½ oz) of the Gruyère or Emmenthal cheese and the Cheddar. Season with a little pepper. Stir this into the pasta. Line a baking tray with non-stick baking parchment and divide the spaghetti into 3 or 4 circles to form the base of the pizzas.

Pre-heat the oven to gas mark 4, 350°F (180°C). Sauté the spring onions and the mushrooms in the butter or margarine for a couple of minutes, then add the chopped tomatoes. Simmer for 4 to 5 minutes and stir in the tomato purée, basil and oregano. Continue to simmer for 3 to 4 minutes. Spread the tomato sauce over the pizza bases, sprinkle over the remaining Gruyère or Emmenthal, the Mozzarella and Parmesan (if using). Bake for 15 to 20 minutes.

makes 3 or 4 individual pizzas

Annabel's baked pizza sandwich

This uses slices of bread instead of pizza dough. It's very simple to make and gets wolfed down by my three children, but there's none left for seconds because Mum usually can't resist helping herself to the fourth portion. You can add some lightly fried mushrooms or chopped peppers to the tomato sauce if you like.

1 onion, peeled and chopped
Olive oil for frying
1 × 400-g (14-oz) tin chopped
tomatoes
2 medium tomatoes, skinned, de-seeded
and chopped
1 teaspoon sugar
1 teaspoon fresh parsley, chopped
½ teaspoon oregano
½ teaspoon dried basil or 1 tablespoon

fresh basil
A little salt and freshly ground black
pepper
6 large slices wheatgerm bread
250 ml (8 fl oz) milk
125 g (4 oz) packet Mozzarella cheese,
sliced
40 g (1½ oz) Parmesan, grated
2 eggs
A knob of butter

Pre-heat the oven to gas mark 4, 350°F (180°C).
Sauté the onion in the oil until soft, then add the chopped tomatoes, fresh tomatoes, sugar, parsley, oregano and basil. Simmer for about 15 minutes and season with salt and pepper. Meanwhile, soak the bread in the milk for 10 to 15 minutes. Arrange two whole and two half slices of bread on the base of an ovenproof dish 20 × 25 cm (8 × 10 in), cover with half of the tomato sauce and top with the slices of Mozzarella cheese. Arrange a second layer of bread slices on top and cover with the rest of the tomato sauce. Beat the egg together with the Parmesan, pour this over the top, dot with butter and prick through the layers with a fork. Bake in the oven for 45 minutes.

makes 4 portions

fish finger pie

Some children are confirmed fish haters but will eat fish fingers so this is a quick and easy way to turn fish fingers into a tasty meal. It's simple to make your own delicious fish fingers – cut a thick fillet of haddock or cod into strips, dip in lightly seasoned beaten egg, then roll in flour and coat in crushed cornflakes. Lightly fry or grill (brushed with melted butter or margerine).

8 fish fingers
1 small onion, peeled and chopped
1 small green pepper, de-seeded and chopped
1 tablespoon vegetable oil

1 × 400-g (14-oz) tin tomatoes or 4 medium tomatoes, skinned, de-seeded and chopped
1 tablespoon tomato purée
75 g (3 oz) Cheddar cheese, grated

Grill or fry the fish fingers until they are cooked. Sauté the onion and green pepper in the oil until soft. Drain the tomatoes, roughly chop them and add to the onion and pepper together with the tomato purée and cook for about 5 minutes. Meanwhile, pre-heat the oven to gas mark 4, 350°F (180°C).

Cut the cooked fish finger into pieces and mix with the tomato sauce. Place in a greased ovenproof dish and cover with the Cheddar or make a cheese sauce. Re-heat in the oven and finish off under the grill.

makes 3 portions

funny face burgers

These are great for a barbecue. You can make each one look different (see illustrations). Alternatively, they could be grilled or fried, served plain or in a bun with some fried onions. I usually make more than I need and put some aside in the freezer (best frozen uncooked and without decoration).

1 medium potato, peeled and grated
450 g (1 lb) lean minced beef
1 onion, peeled and grated
1 large Granny Smith apple, peeled and grated
1 tablespoon chopped fresh parsley
1 chicken stock cube
½ teaspooon Marmite

1 bread roll, made into breadcrumbs, or 50 g (2 oz) breadcrumbs
Mozzarella cheese for the face, grated
Double Gloucester or another orange-coloured cheese, grated, for the hair
Olives or cherry tomatoes or cucumber slices for the eyes
Red pepper for the mouth

Squeeze out the excess liquid from the potatoes. Then mix all the ingredients except the cheeses, olives and pepper together and form into burgers. Barbecue, grill or fry until cooked through. Sprinkle over some Mozzarella for the face and Double Gloucester for hair and place under a hot grill until the cheese melts. Then use the olives etc. to make the faces.

makes about 10 burgers

INDEX

Also by Annabel Karmel

Annabel Karmel's New
Complete Baby and
Toddler Meal Planner
0 09 188088 2

Annabel Karmel's New
Baby and Toddler
Cookbook
0 09 182558 X

Annabel Karmel's
Complete Party Planner
0 09 187526 9

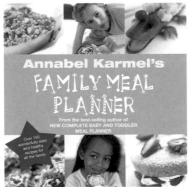

Annabel Karmel's Family
Meal Planner
0 09 186795 9

Annabel Karmel's SuperFoods for
Babies and Children
0 09 187902 7

All are published by Ebury Press and are available from good bookshops
Alternatively, call TBS Direct on 01206 255 800